Chronicle
of a Small Town

A · WARDLAW · BOOK

Chronicle
of a Small Town

ILLUSTRATED BY THE AUTHOR

Jim W. Corder

Texas A&M
University Press
COLLEGE STATION

The paper used in this book meets the minimum requirements
of the American National Standard for Permanence
of Paper for Printed Library Materials, Z39.48-1984.
Binding materials have been chosen for durability.

Library of Congress Cataloging-in-Publication Data
Corder, Jim W. (Jim Wayne), 1929–
    Chronicle of a small town / Jim W. Corder. –
1st. ed.
      p. cm. – (Wardlaw book)
    ISBN 0-89096-414-9 (alk. paper)
    1. Jayton (Tex.) – History. 2. Jayton (Tex.) –
Social life and customs. 3. Corder, Jim W. (Jim
Wayne), 1929– . I. Title. II. Series.
F394.J2C67 1989
976.4'738 – dc20
                                 89-4464
                                    CIP

For Roberta
AND IN MEMORY OF
Ruth Corder (1907–88)
AND
Nolan Corder (1905–88)

Contents

Contents

Publisher's Acknowledgment

The Texas A&M University Press is privileged to add its imprint to this Wardlaw Book. The designation claims a special place in the list of Texas A&M publications.

Supported with funds inspired by the initiative of Chester Kerr, former head of Yale University Press, this book, along with its companion volumes, perpetuates the association of Frank H. Wardlaw's name with a select group of titles appropriate to his reputation as man of letters, distinguished publisher, and founder of three university presses.

Donors of these funds represent a wide cross-section of Frank Wardlaw's admirers, including colleagues from scholarly presses throughout the country as well as those from other callings who recognize and applaud the many contributions that he has made to scholarship, literature, and publishing in his four decades of active service.

The Texas A&M University Press acknowledges with profound appreciation these donors.

Mr. Herbert S. Bailey, Jr.
Mr. Robert Barnes
Mr. W. Walker Cowen
Mr. Robert S. Davis
Mr. John Ervin, Jr.
Mr. William D. Fitch
Mr. August Frugé
Mr. David H. Gilbert
Mr. Kenneth Johnson
Mr. Chester Kerr
Mr. Robert T. King
Mr. Carl C. Krueger, Jr.

Mr. John H. Kyle
John and Sara Lindsey
Mrs. S. M. McAshan, Jr.
Mr. Kenneth E. Montague
Mr. Edward J. Mosher
Mrs. Forence Rosengren
Mr. Jack Schulman
Mr. C. B. Smith
Mr. Richard A. Smith
Mr. Stanley Sommers
Dr. Frank E. Vandiver
Ms. Maud E. Wilcox

Mr. John Williams

Publisher's Acknowledgment

Their bounty has assured that Wardlaw Books will be a special source of instruction and entertainment to the reading public for many years to come.

Chronicle
of a Small Town

1

Subscribing to the *Jayton Chronicle*

I'd been hoping, sometimes casually, sometimes painfully, to find, some way, back issues of the *Jayton Chronicle*, the weekly newspaper of Jayton, Texas, the little town where I spent some years as a boy. I wanted especially to see issues for the years from about 1934 to about 1947, roughly from about the time I would have started remembering until about the time I would have graduated from Jayton High School, if we had still lived in Jayton. I'm blessed if I know exactly why I wanted to see those issues. I thought I would learn why I wanted to see them when I saw them.

Then, in 1983, I went with my father, my brother, and my uncle to Uncle Martin's funeral in Jayton. Uncle Martin and Aunt Mary, my father's sister, hadn't lived in Jayton since the forties, but it was still the burying ground for them. At the funeral, I chanced upon Cornelia Cheyne, or she chanced upon me. Cornelia is the county clerk of Kent County. The courthouse is in Jayton. I have to confess that I didn't remember her, but she seemed to remember me from old times in Jayton. Actually, I think she was remembering my brother better: he is older, and was always given to more sophisticated ways.

At any rate, as we talked I remembered to ask Mrs. Cheyne about the old *Jayton Chronicle*. When I knew it, the paper was published locally and printed in Jayton, and I thought Mr. Wade was the perpetual owner and editor, sufficiently elevated in my mind not to have a first name. But he died, as most do, and change came, and sometime along about 1960, a man from up near Ralls bought up the *Chronicle* and several other little newspapers. He continued publishing them, but all from a central place, with help from local reporters who made their living by holding regular jobs otherwise. At least, that's how I pieced together what happened. In the new manifestation, each little town had its own first page, but the following pages in each weekly issue were identical. In time, that system gave way, too. Now Jayton gets reported by Mrs. Joy Kidd in the *Texas Spur,* twenty-four miles away.

But I wasn't much interested in such recent times, I told Mrs. Cheyne. She told me that she didn't know what had happened to the old newspapers, but promised to ask around.

And she did. Not long afterward, a letter came from her, dated Thursday, October 13:

> Jim I have not had much luck in finding the Jayton Chronicles, but a lady told me that they had copies of it in the Tech Library, South Western Collection, in Lubbock. She said she thought that they were back in the thirties. You can probably call and find out for sure.
>
> The lady called it South Western Collection, but the phone book has it listed as Southwest Collection and their telephone number is Area Code 806-742-3749. The Library–Information Hours telephone number is Area Code 806-742-2251. Hope this helps you find some of what you would like to have. The lady from the paper here said they had a fire and most of what they had was destroyed. We finally got some rain, wasn't enough but sure did help.

Her letter put my mind at ease. They had survived, some at least, and they were on file in a university library where I could find them when I needed them. I put her letter in a place where I could find it and went on working with the projects at hand. The letter made a sweet, warm place in my mind against the time when I could go find the papers, read them, and find out why I had wanted to see them.

Didn't turn out that way.

A few months ago I finished some projects I'd been working on, including some writing about Jayton and kinfolk and dust storms and things. I began to feel itchy again about the *Jayton Chronicle.* Began to seem like it was time.

I called the Southwest Collection at the Texas Tech Library, and spoke to Jan Blodgett. She was helpful, checked the files, and said, yes, they did have a microfilm collection. She asked what years I was interested in, checked again, and when she came back to the phone the news turned sour. After about 1960 the file was complete. Before that time, the file was skimpy—no issues at all for some years, as few as five or six issues each for many years. The file was almost silent on the years I most wanted.

I had depended on the library file for more than three years, had assumed it awaited my convenience. Unwise, to say the least: I lost three years of looking. I felt for a while more than a little sick and guessed once more that everything was gone, blown away like tumbleweeds before the West Texas wind. Some places, they build buildings that stay, and they seem to have archives that keep, and even the landscape seems to stay the way you thought you remembered, not fallen away again before the wind and wasteful rain that comes in driving bunches when you don't need it and in no bunches at all when you do. Nothing much keeps, I thought, and looked some more because there wasn't much else to do.

I talked to the people at the Amon Carter Museum of Western Art in Fort Worth. They have a splendid collection of nineteenth-century newspapers, couldn't help me with the *Jayton Chronicle*, and recommended the Fort Worth Public Library. A kind man there said that they had some papers from Graham, "whatever that is." Actually, I was a little relieved at this—would have been embarrassing if the damned newspapers had been available all along in my own hometown public library.

But, whether from the Carter Museum or the public library, I don't remember, I did learn of another possibility. I called Dr. Bobby Weaver, who directed the Texas Newspaper Project. It's housed in the Panhandle–Plains Historical Museum in Canyon, Texas. The project, as I understand it, is intended both as a repository for small-town newspapers and as a monitor of other files of newspapers. Dr. Weaver checked his files and told me much the same thing I had learned from the Southwest Collection at Texas Tech—few issues before the 1960s were there.

By this time, I had decided that, anyway, I needed to see the Double Mountains and walk the canyons. While I was visiting with my parents before I left, I chanced to tell them about my search for the *Jayton Chronicle*. My mother said, "Well, you know . . ." There was a pause. Then, "Your Aunt Mary might have them. I know she kept them at one time. And she never threw anything away."

It occurred to me that a scholar's reputation, supposing he had one, could be ruined if the world found out that he had discovered his sources at Aunt Mary's house. I called her anyway. She lives in Pecos, Texas. "No," she said, "I don't. I used to keep about a year's worth of them at a time, but that was a long time ago." Then there was a pause. "You know," she said, "Joy Kidd might know something about where copies might be—she lives there in Jayton."

I went on to West Texas, checked in at the Hickman Motel in Aspermont, drove on to Jayton, and hunted up Cornelia Cheyne to find out if she'd had any more thoughts about where old *Chronicles* might be. I told her what I had found at Texas Tech, or what I hadn't

found. Turned out she didn't have any more ideas. I asked her if she knew where I could find Joy Kidd. "Why, you just go out the south door and across the street to the WTU office. She works there."

I did. And she did. I introduced myself, told her I reckoned we were probably kin—my father's mother was Laura Kidd before she was Laura Kidd Corder. I told her my errand, told her I'd been sent by Aunt Mary, Laura Kidd Corder's daughter. We talked for a while, and she thought for a while. I had started for the door that said West Texas Utilities backward when she remembered: "Jerry Parker up at the schoolhouse might know something," she said.

He did.

By this time, I had come to believe that a complete file of the old *Jayton Chronicle* did exist somewhere—I wanted to believe that—but that it lay hidden in someone's attic or closet, not in some public place where I might hear about it and see it. I had come to reckon that I might never see any of the old papers.

But Mr. Parker knew a little. In a small back room in what is still to me the new schoolhouse, mixed in with school files, he had a microfilm collection of the *Jayton Chronicle*—"all," he said, "that I could find." He had microfilmed them himself when they were selling the paper, emptying the old office by the Barfoot Hotel. "A lot of them were gone," he said, "and some that were left were falling apart."

He'd gathered and microfilmed a pretty good collection. One microfilm roll held everything he'd been able to find from 1934 to 1951. I felt pretty good—a single issue of the paper was usually only four or six pages, so you could put quite a few on one roll. I hadn't expected to find a treasure, but thought I had. He's a thoughtful, delightful man,

Mr. Parker, and kind—he let me borrow the microfilm that ran from 1934 to 1951, though not without some hesitation.

But I still didn't have the *Jayton Chronicle*, though it was in my hand. I don't know an awful lot about machines. I thought a microfilm was a microfilm. What Mr. Parker loaned me was a 3M Cartridge Microfilm. When I got back to campus, I went to our library planning to use one of the pretty machines that will let you read the microfilm *and* print out a copy of what's on the screen. Our machines, I discovered, are new, and use only microfilm on reels—they won't accept the cartridge variety. I had been hunting the old *Chronicle* for a long time, had it in my hand, and now couldn't get it out of the cartridge.

I called the Fort Worth Public Library and the local community college. Neither had a machine that liked cartridges. I called the 3M Service Department at 1-800-492-5072 to see if they had files that might tell who in the area owned a compatible reader. They didn't but the lady recommended that I call local microfilm service companies. I did. I called Micro Data Service Center, but they had no machines to hold the cartridge. Neither did Permanent Records, Inc. or Anacomp. A friendly gentleman at Microrecords Service, Inc. told me that he didn't have the right machine, but if necessary would try to rig the cartridge to a machine he had. At ALR Micro-Serv I had more immediate luck: an interesting lady who answered the phone—too nice to treat me as if I were simple-minded—told me how to take the cartridge apart, to run its insides onto a reel, and then to put it all back again.

And that's what I'm going to do this afternoon, Mr. Parker, but not if it seems likely to harm the record you made for the rest of us.

The cartridge is on my desk now. I know how to get inside it, and the machines in the library will make copies for me. I don't know exactly what Mr. Parker's identifying label means, and I don't know exactly how much there is inside the cartridge. There's something there for 1934, 1937, 1938, 1939, 1942, 1943, 1945, and 1946. I'll go this afternoon and look. I'm afraid of what I won't find. I'm afraid of what I will find.

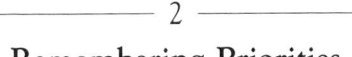

2

Remembering Priorities

I can't seem to keep priorities straight. Some people seem able to do so. I knew a young man once who had a "game plan"—his phrase, not mine – for his life. He always seemed to know which way was north, which end was up, and what to do first. He knows how to "prioritize" – his word, not mine – his chores. He always seems to know which way the wind is blowing, where the bottom line is, and what to do first. I'm seldom sure.

Well, maybe that's not accurate. I do have some sense of priorities, except that I tend to list in first place everything that isn't done with a shovel or a machine. At any rate, I have over the years tried to do different kinds of work – sometimes, I have to say, simultaneously, which doesn't turn out too well. I don't need to be congratulated for that: I should have done more and better, and should, besides, have kept a better yard and garden.

Some of this work I couldn't avoid – it's what I do for a living. I've used diverse terms for diverse work. Sometimes I've thought of myself as *working* (that is, for a living) and *doing honest work* (that is, doing the work that pleases me most). Sometimes I've thought of myself as doing one kind of work with the right hand, another with the left, though I'm not always sure which is which. Actually, of course, the two kinds of work are not all that different. The work I do for a monthly check often entails writing. The work I do with my other hand always entails writing. Both kinds of writing, oftener than not, rise out of surprise, out of memory confounded.

Surprise didn't cease when I began reading the *Jayton Chronicle*, and memory was often bewildered. I found the microfilm file of the paper on January 30, 1987, at the hand of Jerry Parker of the Jayton Independent School District. From the first, I had resolved not just to read the microfilm image enlarged on the screen, but to make, as they say, "hard copy" of each page, and so I regularly went to the library to sit before the magic machine, once I learned how to transform Mr. Parker's cartridge into a reel. I put the reel on the machine, which then showed me the *Jayton Chronicle*, page by page on the screen, and when I dropped a dime into the machine, it would also produce a paper copy of the image on the screen.

The going was slow, for two reasons. In the first place, my eyes don't adjust easily to the light of a microfilm reader, and often I was able to do only fifty or sixty pages a day, or ten to fifteen issues of the *Chronicle*. As a consequence, I didn't finish making hard copies until March 16. The second reason I was slow was that, though I had planned to wait for hard copy to pore over, I couldn't resist reading from the screen as I copied, and so I began to learn before I began to learn.

What I learned was often, if not continually, surprising. That wouldn't have startled me, I guess, if I had remembered that memory is unreliable, if I hadn't kept in my mind images of Jayton that I was certain were accurate, except that they turned out not to be. I'm reasonably sure what Jayton looks like now—I was there looking some six weeks ago. I *thought* I knew what it looked like then, say in spring or summer, 1938, or maybe 1939, but I didn't have it all right.

For example. Imagine that I'm standing at the northwest corner of the square before it was split by the new highway, long before it was largely given over to the new courthouse when Clairemont gave up and the county seat was moved to Jayton. Imagine that I'm standing at the northwest corner of the square, looking to the north. This is what I *knew* I would see, not now, but then; now, it's all different.

The street that I always thought of as Main Street (I don't know that it had a name) runs along the west side of the square and on to the north where I imagine myself looking. The first building on the corner on the left side of the street is what I remember as Gardner's Grocery. The front is tall, perhaps a false front, with an awning out over the sidewalk that begins at the corner by the grocery and runs on by the other buildings on that side. The Texas Theater is next, with TEXAS in big letters and two small billboards and a recessed box office. The front, at least, is two stories tall—you know how they do theaters so the projectionist can be up there above the lobby. Beyond the the-

ater is Huls Drug Store in a two-story building with a doctor's office and I don't know what else upstairs. Across the street on the corner, but facing south onto the square, is Jones Drug Store. Up the street to the north past these buildings, in my mind, there is nothing much — an abandoned service station, then open space, the Baptist church, then homes, all on the left, nothing on the right.

But it wasn't exactly like that. As I was making copies, I kept stopping to read from the screen, not carefully but frequently, and I kept learning things before I set out to read the hard copies slowly and carefully. I can't recapture exactly what the buildings looked like; the *Chronicle* issues before me carried no pictures. But I found that I had some things wrong, though I knew I was right. The Texas Theater wasn't the TEXAS. Advertisements in the *Chronicle* showed me that for a while it was the PALACE, then the KENT, then the TEXAN. I was certain that there were no buildings behind Jones Drug Store, but advertisements informed me that at one time, while my family was there, the Green Castle Cafe did business in that spot.

Jones Drug Store housed a few shelves of books that constituted the town library, and I had always known that the town undertaking establishment was in the back of the store. It wasn't. Undertaking was undertaken in the back of Mr. Charlie Robinson's grocery and hardware and clothing store over on the east side of the square. His regular advertisements in 1934 carry the motto, "Everything From the Cradle to the Grave." How could I not have known that, or known it and forgotten? Mr. Charlie Robinson was an important personage, the father of sweet, red-haired Peggy Sue, whom I loved deeply from afar until my family moved away in late 1939, when we parted forever in the fourth grade, though I'm not at all certain that she noticed.

Along the way I've clearly and quite without knowing it given priority to some things and kept them, though wrong, in memory, but have devalued others and lost them. Why did I remember things one way when all along they were another way? And what else did I get wrong?

I've tried to understand what there is about my thinking that would cause or lead me to remember some things but not others and to remember some things wrong, but I have only partial explanations. I remember being in the grocery story on the corner and so have associated though scattered images that would help me keep it in mind. But I would never have been in or thought about the Green Castle Cafe. I was never in a cafe in those days. We didn't have money, and besides, one didn't eat out so readily in that time and place. Eating out was wasteful and might signify that you couldn't get a decent meal together at home.

I don't know why I misremembered the name of the theater, but it's clear to my why I would remember the theater itself — it was a magical place, after all, though I didn't get to go all that often. The times when my family could afford a dime for a picture show and the times when various owners could afford to keep the theater open did not always coincide. But it was a wondrous place. I saw some but not all episodes of a Tailspin Tommy serial there and some of the episodes of "The Mark of Zorro," and once an old gentlemen appeared there who said he was Jesse James, and had just come out of his long hiding and that dirty little coward hadn't killed him after all. He had long white hair and a white beard. He wore a black hat and a long black coat and black pants and, I think, a white shirt, and he had two pearl-handled pistols hung low on his hips.

A special memory calls back Huls Drug Store. I remember only one visit, but it was splendid. For some reason I was downtown with my Grandpa. It was, as I call it back, a summer day, fiercely bright and hot, and I had a blind, desperate headache. My Grandpa decided that what I needed was to get into a cool, shady place and have a Coca-Cola. We went into Huls Drug Store and sat at the fountain, and I had my first experience of fountain cola and was cured.

Some places, in other words, became present to me, and I remembered them, even if sometimes erroneously. Other places didn't, and I didn't.

But I may have had other priorities all along that I didn't know about and can scarcely guess at now. The grocery store, the theater, the drug store—all gone now—were or seemed to be two-story structures, taller than Jones Drug across the street and taller than the buildings that must have housed the Green Castle Cafe and who knows what else. Perhaps I was never in control of memory. Recent neurological and brain-mapping research suggests that we remember verticals better and longer than we remember horizontals. Did I remember the grocery store, the theater, the drug store only or chiefly because they were taller than all the other buildings, taller, I think, than everything in Jayton except the water tower to the south and the oil mill to the east?

I don't know. I thought I had it pictured right. I didn't. I wanted to get things right, have them fixed.

I can't. I'll read the *Chronicle.*

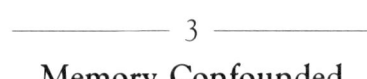

3

Memory Confounded

Well, the truth is, dammit, I didn't even get that little part right. Before I finished making copies of the *Jayton Chronicle,* I kept on glancing at the screen, seeing headlines, sometimes reading parts of articles and noticing advertisements; and well before I sat down to study the copies I had made, I discovered that I still didn't have it straight about Mr. Robinson, or about sweet Peggy Sue. Mr. Charlie Robinson was an important person, to be sure. He did own the grocery–hardware–dry goods store on the east side of the square, with undertaking in the back, to provide all one's needs from the cradle to the grave, but he wasn't Peggy Sue's father. I finally came across an item as I read the screen image of the *Chronicle* that made me remember. Peggy Sue's father was Mr. Baker Robinson, known as Bake, and brother to Mr. Charlie Robinson. Mr. Charlie Robinson's daughter was Lucille. Peggy Sue's older brother was Red Robinson, my brother's best friend.

I guess I didn't even remember sweet Peggy Sue all that well. In the *Jayton Chronicle* for December 8, 1938, a little story says that Peggy Sue and I had the leading roles in the third grade Christmas play that was presented before the whole school. Says so right there in the paper, but I don't remember it at all. I'd swear to God I didn't do it.

4

Confounded Memory

I have a photograph of a little rock house. I took it twenty-some years ago on a trip with my family. Recently, I tried making some ink sketches from the photograph. One of them turned out all right if you sort of squint your eyes when you look at it. While I was in Jayton on the same trip that finally led to Mr. Parker and the *Jayton Chronicle*, I tried to find the little rock house again, as I had tried on other visits. I can't find it.

I think I've been on the right road, but I can't find it. Perhaps it's gone. When I saw it that time, it was long since a ruin, a shell, but the rocks were good. Maybe someone needed the rocks. Rocks hold on longer.

During that same trip twenty-some years ago, when I first and last saw the house, I chanced to mention it to my Aunt Edith. She shuddered, remembered the house, and said she didn't want to think about it. She'd lived in that house with a family during her first year of teaching in the early 1930s, and it was dark and lonely, and the wind moaned between the rocks. The little house was not much larger than

our living room, but she'd lived there with a family. She was the teacher at the Golden Pond School, deep in the Croton Breaks, miles from Jayton or anywhere. I've found Golden Pond. The shell of one building and a small cemetery remain. In the summer the weeds are high and thick in the cemetery.

Some time after that conversation with Aunt Edith, I asked my parents about Edith's experience. Edith is my mother's sister. They remembered her time at Golden Pond as hard, harder than I guessed. She had been away to college for one year in Denton, at what we now call Texas Woman's University, but which was then called, I believe, the College of Industrial Arts. She came back to West Texas and took her first job as a teacher at age seventeen at Golden Pond, but had to work without pay until she was eighteen and legal, or so my parents remembered. What she got instead of pay was board and room in that little rock house.

But then recently, almost twenty-some years later, I asked my parents about Edith's experience again. Now they're not sure where she taught, though they remember that she was seventeen.

I can't get stories, or the world, straight.

I can't find the little house, though I have found the remnant of Golden Pond, but now they can't be sure that's where she taught.

I can't get stories, or the world, straight, or find the little rock house. I didn't have it right about undertaking in Jayton, or about the Green Castle Cafe. I didn't have Mr. Charlie Robinson and Mr. Bake Robinson straight in my mind, or sweet Peggy Sue, and I'm damned if I can remember the third-grade Christmas play.

If I can't get a few memories straight, or a little rock house, or a little town, or the name of a theater, how am I going to get the world, or myself, straight? A fellow ought to be able to count a little on former experience as a guide—but I sometimes misremember former experience, and besides, it's usually inadequate to present need.

Meanwhile, am I only a misperception, a failed memory in the mind of someone else?

———— 5 ————

What Was on the Microfilm

I found more than I expected, but less than I had hoped. I didn't go all the way to the end of Mr. Parker's microfilm. I didn't want to. Were you expecting disinterested history?

If I had gone to the end, the microfilm would have taken me past scattered issues to 1951. I stopped with the last available paper of the years I was interested in, that for December 12, 1946. I don't know whether I can explain why. I'm pretty sure that I can't explain why, at least not entirely. When you set out to explain or to probe, soon you come up against what you can't know.

I stopped with the issue for December 12, 1946, because by that time I was thinking about other things. I had been graduated from high school in June, 1946, a year ahead of what would have been my Jayton class. Perhaps Jayton prepared me better (or worse) than I know: after my family moved to the big city, I skipped the fifth grade and so graduated ahead of those in my class at Jayton. By December, 1946, I was thinking about other things, and they were ready to be graduated. By 1946, Jayton seemed strange, lost to me, and I was a stranger to Jayton. The ending of what would have been my school years there seemed to afford a neat place to stop, so I quit reading Mr. Parker's microfilm. I assumed, for right or wrong, that any I had known there would soon scatter.

Then what was on the microfilm?

When I finished making copies from the microfilm, I had copies of 241 issues of the weekly *Jayton Chronicle*. My first copy is dated January 5, 1934; the last is dated December 12, 1946. Except for fewer than ten, they are complete. Those few that weren't complete had missing or torn pages. The microfilm actually began with a stutter. The first issue shown was for November 28, 1934, out of place. Then there were five half-pages with no dates. Then came the issue for January 5, 1934, and after that the issues were shown chronologically, with gaps large and small. The dates are not always exactly a week apart, though mostly: once in a while, Mr. Wade shifted from Thursday to Friday publication, and to Wednesday before Thanksgiving Day. I have copies of 241 issues — might have been better, might have been worse.

For 1934, I have forty issues. All of August is missing. All of December is missssing. A few scattered weeks otherwise are missing.

For 1935, there were no issues. I wondered what news I had missed. I cannot ever reclaim the news exactly.

For 1936, there were no issues. I wondered what news I had missed. I cannot ever reclaim the news exactly. For 1936, there were no issues on the microfilm. I wondered what news I had missed, what memories were wrong. I cannot ever reclaim the news exactly. The *Jayton Chronicle* may not have had the news exactly right either.

For 1937, I have thirty-four issues. Most of the January and April issues are missing. All of the May issues are missing. Two weeks of both June and August are missing, and a few scattered weeks otherwise.

For 1938, I have forty-four papers. Three weeks are missing in August, three in late September through mid-October. Otherwise, scattered single issues are missing. The record is mostly nearly complete in 1938.

Following the 1938 issues were five entries — duplicates of papers already shown and fragments.

For 1939, I have forty-two issues of the *Jayton Chronicle*. Those for September 21 and September 28 are reversed on the microfilm. All of November, 1939, is missing, and most of December, and a few scattered issues otherwise.

When I found that the issues for November, 1939, were missing, I felt a small chill along my back, or something that required me to shake my shoulders. I think my family left Jayton in November, 1939 — I think but do not know, and haven't gone to inquire, for other people's memories are scarcely more reliable than mine. I think I'm right, though.

My brother stayed behind in Jayton for a couple of weeks to be in the class play. I found no mention of the play in the paper. In other years, there is ample notice in the *Chronicle* of play presentations at the school auditorium, so I think it must have happened in November—the play, the paper's announcement of it, and our departure—in November, that is, the missing November. I didn't expect my family's move to be announced, but I did feel funny down my back when I found November gone.

All of the issues for 1940 are missing.

All of the issues for 1941 are missing.

But I have forty-two papers from 1942. Some of January is missing. Two different papers are dated April 9, 1942. One of them must be the issue for April 2, 1942, which doesn't show otherwise. Scattered weeks are missing, and all of December, 1942, is gone.

I have only one paper for 1943, that for April 8.

For 1944, there were no issues.

For 1945, I have twenty-nine papers. All of January and most of February are missing. March and April and scattered other weeks are missing.

I have nine papers from 1946, one for January, two for February, one for April, one for August, three for September, and the last, for December 12, where I stopped.

I have 241 issues of the *Jayton Chronicle*.

6

Time Is Gone and History Is Uncertain

In the thirteen years I was most interested in, from 1934 through 1946, there might have been, probably were, 676 papers, assuming there were 52 each year. I have 241 issues. Of the possible issues of the *Jayton Chronicle* in those thirteen years, there are 435 that I do not have.

As I read the *Jayton Chronicle*, sometimes surprised by the news, by news I had not known, by news that I remembered so surely and so wrong, I found myself wondering, again and again, what I would have learned, what would have startled me, what I could have seen in a new way that I had misremembered, if only I could read *the missing papers*. There are always missing papers.

——— 7 ———
Methodology

I had thought at first to say that there was no method to my study of the *Jayton Chronicle* except to root around, browse, look, and see what I learned as I went along. I still think that's a reasonable account of what I did. I also know that it is not a faithful account. My mind didn't shut down until I finished reading all of the papers. Having the papers in my hand kept Jayton in my mind. I thought about those times, and myself, after I read the papers and while I was reading them and before I read them.

By some standards, that's laxity beyond pardon. Such attitudes as I have toward experience—old experience, old experience retold, new experience found in the *Chronicle*—yield effects that some would find immeasurable and unreliable; shaky opinion, not fact. They're probably right. I haven't found the facts yet and probably won't. I don't know that the *Chronicle* owns the facts either.

Still, some think that if research is specific and if it is guided by an appropriate research methodology, it will yield generalizable findings —not opinion, but conclusions derived from research. In my regular work—when I'm not reading the *Jayton Chronicle*—that kind of work is granted status, authority, reliability, believability. Writing that is regarded as "commentary" or "opinion" is sometimes separated from valorized "research findings." I'm not always able to make such distinctions or to know what the facts are.

George Will seemed to have it right about facts the other day in his column. Writing about the Supreme Court's action to strike down Louisiana's law requiring the teaching of "creation science" where evolution is taught, he noted the unwillingness of some to confront facts; said "there is no scientific 'debate' about whether evolution is a fact," and "evolution is a fact about which there are various explanatory theories"; and he defined facts as "revisable data about the world."

That made sense to me—I've often enough revised the data I had about the world, and have certainly told stories as gospel truth only to discover that I didn't have things quite right. I agreed with him altogether about the folly of something called "creation science," thought he was entirely right in his judgment that fundamentalists would not face evidence, and remained disturbed, not by his views, but by my own over in my little world. I can't get facts straight.

Have I got the facts yet about Mr. Charlie Robinson and Mr. Bake Robinson? And what about the Coffee Pot Cafe and the Green Castle Cafe? And the high school football team that I had wrong? I don't think so. I'm learning, but I haven't got it straight yet. If facts are "revisable data about the world," are they interpretations, judgments, opinions, found after thought and search, facts being facts as best they can according to the thought of the day?

It seems so to me, uncomfortably, even while I know that to think so is to authorize others to take their crazy-headed unevidenced prejudices as fact. The difference, I guess, is in what we take to be evidence and whether or not we're willing to look. If I think for forty years that mortuary work was done in the back of Jones Drug, I can learn from the advertisements that it wasn't, that Mr. Robinson did it. If I want to think in 1938 that Jews are disease-carrying vermin or in 1987 that earth was created in 4004 B.C., the *Jayton Chronicle* won't tell me otherwise and I won't be willing to look at any rate.

I wanted to think that I would get the facts, the fixed whole truth, or at least a piece of it that was certain—wanted, as Ellen Bryant Voight says in "The Lotus Eater,"

> to salvage
> something from my life, to fix
> some truth beyond all change.

I'm not sure that I will. Things, people, events slip away. I can't elevate my musings, or even what I learn from reading, to assurance, will never to able to testify that I have all the facts. In the end, I'll be pretty sure that certain things happened on certain days, and I'll have some opinions.

Opinions, of course, can be silly, trivial, evil, and I certainly can't elevate mine to assurance. I know that we often treat our opinions— and our memories—as if they were authoritative, both for ourselves and for others as we tell them our tales. Poor substitutes they are for whatever the truth may be, but they're mostly what we have, tentatively or otherwise, as truth, and can rise not just from thoughtless perpetuation of prejudice and faulty memory, but also from such study and thought as we can manage.

Research, too, is opinion and interpretation at last. No research methodology is divine; none is the sole route to truth. A research methodology is a human rhetoric that lets us create structures of meaning. Such rhetorics are not in the nature of things; they are the spoken, written, created nature of things, deriving from the utterances of a community, much as facts become factual through the agreement of an assenting community. Knowledge is not a sacred finding, forever fixed, but the product, temporal and temporary, of human insight and judgment.

(Sometimes, probably too often, we teach students to imagine that knowledge is forever fixed, a collection of discrete parts, and they come to suppose, as we apparently do, that "objective" tests are the appropriate measure of an "objective" factual world. All the right answers must be the same for every student; the knowledge tested for is abstract, impersonal, universally acknowledged. Such tests assume that knowledge is fixed and eternal, independent of the knower, and independent of language. We hide our interpretations and opinions, or rename them, turning them into objective, reliable facts through a presumably authenticating test — or a research methodology.)

And yet. And yet. I wanted to think I could catch Jayton — or myself in Jayton, or somewhere — and get some things fixed, certain. I've told enough accounts of my childhood that were, however entertaining and folksy, thoroughly unreliable. But I probably won't escape that. I can try to hold personal experience in some balance with what I read in the *Chronicle,* and hope that they once in a while match, but in the end what I'll have is what gets into my head, and I have no methodology that will elevate that to assurance. I can tell what I think I know. I can try to remember that most sentences — probably all sentences, including those in scientific papers — ought to begin with "As I understand matters, . . ." "As I see it, . . ." and end with ". . . or so it seems to me."

Methodologies, so it seems to me, may not take mysteries into account. Questions occur that I might not, would not, have anticipated. Four young men from the area died in action during World War II (at least one other died in training, and there may have been others, whether in training or in action, that I missed): H. J. Whatley in a Japanese prison camp, Curtis Hancock and Jeff Brown in combat air missions, Gatlin Cox in infantry fighting near the end of the war in the Philippines. After the war was over, I'm told in the *Jayton Chronicle* for February 21, 1946, the American Legion post in Jayton was named the Whatley-Hancock Post. Why wasn't it named the Cox-Brown Post, or the Whatley-Hancock-Cox-Brown Post? The newspaper doesn't tell me. How the hell am I supposed to know? In the cemetery, the stones don't tell me. I find Whatley and Brown and Hancock, but not Cox. Where is he?

Earlier, I had thought it was simpler.

I unscrewed Mr. Parker's cartridge, bared the tape, and wound it on a reel that Ms. Wittemeyer supplied. She is the periodicals librarian for the campus where I work.

She showed me the machine (actually, there were two) in a cubicle just off the periodicals reading room where I could insert the reel I'd made and wind it out, page by page. As each page came up on the screen, I could read it or, if I inserted a dime, make a copy, or I could do both. From early February to March 16, 1987, I did both, usually making copies of no more than fifty to sixty pages at a sitting, unable to resist reading the screen images, though I had resolved to wait for the printed copies.

Slowly, I accumulated pages. When I finished, I had 241 issues of the *Jayton Chronicle*, or something like twelve hundred pages. The printed images were mostly eight and a half by eleven inches, though sometimes I used the other machine that gave six by eight and a half–inch images. When I had finished, I bound the near twelve hundred pages into four gatherings.

That much done, I thought that I would read 241 issues of the *Jayton Chronicle* to see what I learned. Earlier, I had thought it was simpler. I thought I should first set down a little chronology of my life as a boy in Jayton, with such memories as I could catch, and I have done that (in the section following this one). This small history, I thought, might give me something to measure against as I learned the news in the *Chronicle*, perhaps found surprises there. Seemed simpler when I started: I would write a little chronology from my recollections and, against that, measure what I learned from the *Chronicle*. But I found my plans often interrupted and myself surprised.

I kept remembering the issues I didn't have, some 435, and wondering what I might have learned from them.

I didn't come to the *Jayton Chronicle* empty-headed. What was already there got in the way. Along the way, I hope I've come to know, as Clara Claiborne Park says, that "history is both more complicated and more interesting than that historical sediment that settles into received myths and collective fictions"–or into my mind. And I know, as Park continues, that "the familiar texts, looked at without preconceptions, will give us, if possible, even greater respect for the wisdom, breadth, sophistication, and humanity of our forefathers and leave us with even less respect for our own self-congratulatory simplifications."

I was already interested–that's why I had hunted the *Chronicle*.

Peter Brooks remarks in *Reading for the Plot* that "our lives are ceaselessly intertwined with narrative, with the stories that we tell and hear told, those we dream or imagine or would like to tell, all of which are re-worked in that story of our own lives that we narrate to ourselves in an episodic, sometimes semiconscious, but virtually uninterrupted mono-logue. We live immersed in narrative, recounting and reassessing the meaning of our past actions, anticipating the outcome of our future proj-ects, situating ourselves at the intersection of several stories not yet com-pleted." I didn't come to the *Jayton Chronicle* empty-headed. I had already written a little about Jayton and West Texas. I had already lived there long ago, and wondered about it since. I couldn't resist reading the im-ages on the screen as I was making copies, finding new bits and pieces, caught especially by accounts of events at school, by news of the foot-ball team I thought I remembered, by notice of my grandfather's death.

And so, when I set out to read, to take notes from the *Chronicle*, to try to be systematic, I was already looking for some things and prob-ably not seeing other things. Sometimes, you can't see what is not in your vocabulary to look for. When I set out to read the *Chronicle*, I was, I believe, looking for news, for what I didn't know—I knew so little, and wanted to know a lot.

I started looking early on at the advertisements, could not avoid looking at them, and they alerted me, again and again, to notice the distances, the great stretches of space and time, between the world I'm in now in 1987 and the world I may have been in in 1934 or 1937 or 1938 or 1942. I was, of course, looking to find validation of my mem-ory of those years—and, as I quickly began to see in the images of the *Chronicle* that my memory was wrong, that I had things all wrong, I began to look for surprise, for what I had wrong. And I was looking for myself.

I don't find it discouraging—or wrong—that I was already inter-ested before I started. I was interested. That is to say, I had an interest. Friends and colleagues, to be sure, have recommended a *disinterested* approach to study, a scientific approach, an appropriately designed em-pirical approach to study. Not long ago, the day's mail included a bro-chure announcing an academic conference and calling for papers to be submitted and reviewed for presentation at the conference. "A paper should report on specific research," the brochure said, and "include a description of research methodology." Among the other stipulations was this: "Papers offering opinion, rather than conclusions derived from re-search, are discouraged."

I was discouraged. I'm not able to mark clearly the line between opinion on the one hand and, on the other, conclusions derived from research. The chemist of 1987 is already interested, having already accepted, unless he or she is revolutionary, contemporary metaphors for chemical descriptions. I expect that a historian may be disinterested in a particular subject, area, person, event, or chronology that he or she writes about; but that historian, interested in writing history with all the cultural assumptions that entails, has already accepted some model for writing history.

We are not finished yet, and don't manage to say the final truth, for we are not authorities. What we say has to be revised. We make a little knowledge as we go and share it when we can, recognizing that it is incomplete and will probably remain so. Things don't get fixed and stay fixed. I don't think we should expect them to, though I often do. Whoever looks at what I look at will see it in a different way and tell about it in a different way, and we needn't — can't — purge our thoughts of that subjectivity: we're going to see the world through whatever interpretive scheme our history has given us for seeing the world, and should, I think, repudiate the tyranny of any model over our conceptions of fact and knowledge, should reject any singular, univocal authority. We might learn, someday, to rejoice a little over what we are or can learn to be — poor frail humans, provisional self-makers, provisional world-makers, always awaiting revision.

But I am, of course, troubled by my own views. Will we ever see? Will we want to see? Will our own eyes keep us from seeing?

In his poem, "This Morning," Raymond Carver tells about a morning that "was something":

> A little snow
> lay on the ground. The sun floated in a clear
> blue sky. The sea was blue, and blue-green,
> as far as the eye could see.
> Scarcely a ripple. Calm.

The speaker in the poem dressed and went for a walk, "determined not to return / until I took in what Nature had to offer," saw "old, bent-over trees," crossed a field "strewn with rocks / where snow had drifted," then

> Kept going
> until I reached the bluff.
> Where I gazed at the sea, and the sky, and
> the gulls wheeling over the white beach

far below. All lovely. All bathed in a pure
cold light. But, as usual, my thoughts
began to wander. I had to will
myself to see what I was seeing
and nothing else. I had to tell myself *this* is what
mattered, not the others. (And I did see it,
for a minute or two!) For a minute or two
it crowded out the usual musings on
what was right, and what was wrong — duty,
tender memories, thoughts of death, how I should treat
my former wife. All the things
I hoped would go away this morning.
The stuff I live with every day. What
I've trampled on in order to stay alive.

I resolved to sit down and to read the *Jayton Chronicle.*
But that's not quite true, either.

I had 241 issues, somthing over twelve hundred pages. I didn't read everything, not at first. I may not read everything at last, either. When I sat down to be systematic, I didn't start with the first page and read through to the last. Instead, I looked at every page and, judging from the headline and opening paragraph, marked each item I wanted to come back to for slow and careful reading. On the first run-through, I chose not to pay particular attention to the advertisements, though I could not help seeing what a different world they showed — no, a startling world — and I'll come back to them. As I marked the news items for closer, slower reading, sure enough they began to fall into noticeable groups. I was sorting and grouping before I realized I was sorting and grouping — and what wonders and mysteries do you suppose I have left out by sorting and grouping?

I marked items that told about town activities — women's clubs, men's clubs, church work, campaigns for road improvement. I marked items that told about places — buildings, cafes, places I knew, places I didn't know. I watched especially for news of football, basketball, softball, and my brother. I marked the "Personals" for news of those I knew and those I didn't know. I looked for references to kinfolks, family, myself. I checked most or all items that referred to the Jayton School. I looked for Grandpa Corder when he died. I marked items about the picture show; it changed ownership and name frequently. I watched for signs of the times — depression, unemployment, sheriff's sales, relief checks, soil conservation, the need for trench silos and terracing, notice of the year's cotton crop and when the first bale came in, records of rain and the need for rain, more often records of dust storms. I looked for changes in journalistic practice. And I watched the ads.

I wish I had the papers for the fall of 1936. Reports must have shown that the cotton crop was poor, the number of bales down. All I know now is that the oil mill closed down early, and my father was out of work. The oil mill depended entirely on the cotton crop, and used it up entirely. The mill started up maybe in August, maybe as late as October, whenever the cotton seeds were sent over after the gin was through with them. First, my father said, they ginned the seeds all over again to get the remaining fuzz off—they called it *linters*. The linters got baled up like cotton and was sold for padding and cheap mattresses, but mostly went to munitions plants to make packing for shells. Then they hulled the seeds, rolled them, and put them in big cookers, and when the seeds were cooked and soft, they went into the presses, and the hydraulics would squeeze the hot oil out of them. The caked seeds were broken up into meal and sold for cattle feed. The hulls often became fertilizer. The oil went off somewhere to turn into Crisco. Hulls, linters, seed, oil—they used the cotton seeds up altogether.

But it didn't take long in 1936. The mill closed early—I don't know when, maybe late 1936, or very early 1937. My father found work with the Highway Department. They were finishing the new road between Jayton and Spur. We moved to a little house not far from Grandpa Durham's farm, maybe five miles outside of Spur. My brother and I rode the school bus into Spur for the rest of that year, the first grade for me. I guess we moved back to Jayton in the summer of 1937. I don't know. I can't catch it all. I mark items in the newspapers, but new events and mysteries occur that I hadn't imagined. Events, Wyatt Prunty says in his poem "Room Without Walls" turn into

> . . . a daguerreotype
> Fading and slightly out of focus.

I mark items in the *Chronicle*, but I can't catch it all. Prunty says in "To My Father":

> No cartography could get you here,
> No bread crumbs get you back . . .

The past is always edited by memory. Memory picks and chooses, not always well. I can't find it all.

— 8 —
Back to the Beginning, Or to Very Little

Earlier, I thought I should first get down a little chronology of my life as a boy in Jayton, with such memories as I could catch. This small history, I thought, might give me something to measure against as I learned the news in the *Chronicle*, perhaps found surprises there.

The trouble was, when I came to do it, to write the little chronology, I couldn't. I didn't know much, couldn't get months, years, people, events straight, owned only jumbled images of Jayton.

I thought I knew some things, have told stories to others as if I knew things. I mostly didn't. Reading the *Jayton Chronicle*, I've learned to doubt much that I thought I knew, though Mr. Wade probably didn't set out to teach me this lesson.

My family came to Jayton in 1934, I guess—I don't know and haven't asked. My parents had lived in Jayton or the area before, but had been away to Munday and Rule and I don't know where else.

Kent County and Jayton lie in what the 1933 *Texas Almanac* (I couldn't find the one for 1934) called the "Lower West Texas Prairies"; the area lies

> between the West Cross–Timbers and the foot of the great plains on the east and west and extends from the Red River on the north approximately to the Colorado on the south. It extends across the Red River into Western Oklahoma and there is a fringe lying along the eastern part of the Panhandle below the Cap Rock.
>
> The surface is one of undulating plains with relatively little timber, traversed by the many main channels and tributaries of the Colorado, Brazos, Trinity and Red Rivers. The rainfall varies from about 30 to 20 inches and the climate varies from mild to middle temperate. The elevation ranges approximately from 1,000 to 3,000 feet. The breaks below the cap rock approach the mountainous and there are isolated eminences where an extra thickness of cap rock has shielded areas from erosion, forming ranges of low, flat-topped mountains.

Kent County was created in 1876, named for Andrew Kent, a hero of the Alamo, and it was organized in 1892. The area is 875 square miles. Population reported in 1933 was 3,851, or 4.4 per square mile, not crowded. The almanac says the county is "rolling plain short distance below cap rock escarpment at altitude of about 2,000 to 2,800 feet. Rainfall, 22.72 in. Loam and sandy loam soils." The county was apparently producing an average of 12,500 bales of cotton per year. Clairemont was still the county seat. The almanac reports that there were 831 families in the county, 329 home owners, 478 tenants, and 443 registered vehicles. Kent County doesn't show up in reports of oil production. In 1930, five income tax returns were registered for the county. The scholastic population, upon which the state based its apportionment, was 1,063. Jayton showed a population of 623, with thirty-five business enterprises.

My family came to Jayton, I guess, in 1934. I was maybe four years old.

I have one or two quick snapshots in my head of Seymour, where we had lived before, but they are fuzzy and brown around the edges. The first house I remember in Jayton was next door to my grandparents' house, not too far west of the square, just down the right-field foul line from the softball diamond that's not there any more, and there was a fig tree, and there was trouble somehow when Uncle Carl was drunk and maybe hit Aunt Lizzie and Grandpa raged somehow, and there was a hammer, but they stopped him. The house isn't there any more, and my grandparents' house is not there any more.

The second house I can remember living in (I think it must have been for only a short while) was not far from the northeast corner of the square. It is not there any more, and I can scarcely remember it at all, except for Mr. Meador telling stories, except for the abandoned and rusted tank that lay on its side across the dirt road. It was big enough for club meetings, if I'd had a club.

The third house is gone, too, the Jay house by the dairy, on I think the northeast edge of town, where we lived in half a house, maybe just for a little while, but I cannot remember it or picture it, except that there was heavy wood and leather furniture in the other half.

Then it was fall, 1936, and I started school. My teacher was Mayme Morris Murphy, but then she got married and was Mayme Morris Murphy Fowler. By then we lived in what I've thought of since as the shotgun house, three narrow rooms in a row, in the southeast corner of town. I remember the wood stove in our living room, where I guess my brother and I must also have slept. In a temper fit or something—maybe because he dared me—I shot the boy down the road in the leg with a BB gun and ran home and stayed close to my mother and expected the sheriff to come. The house is gone.

But the drought was bad and cotton was sparse, so the oil mill closed down, and my father found work with the Highway Department, building the new highway to Spur. We moved to a small house in the country some four or five miles outside Spur, some two or three miles from my other grandparents' farm. The house had two rooms, and there was a little shed out back, and off to the northwest I could see the outcropping where my father and the others were crushing rock for gravel to make the highway. My brother and I trapped a rabbit in the culvert, killed it with rocks, and my mother skinned and cooked the thing for us to eat.

My brother and I walked maybe half a mile across a mesquite pasture to catch the school bus. Once we missed the bus, and a man in a car stopped to offer us a ride, but we were virtuous about strangers and turned him down, and I guess my mother was watching because she was pretty mad at us for not getting on in to school. As punishment she said we had to take a couple of jars of peaches or something to my grandmother at the farm, and so we set off, walking, we two, and suffered a whole lot that day—loafing and eating with Grandma and Grandpa.

Once, that spring, I stayed home from school sick, and a hard, dark dust storm blew in, though the sun was still there above. That afternoon, when my brother got off the bus and started home, the dust was blowing so hard that he lost his way and had to backtrack to find home. Later, he swore to me that the sun was shining above the dust and the dust was thick and he saw his shadow in the air beside him and I believed him, and I still do, and the image of my brother's shadow in the air has stayed in my eyes and mind since, and will forever.

The house is still there. I found it again on Saturday, July 26, 1986. The little porch has fallen into a tangle of gray and broken and rotted planks. Sunlight scatters through the roof into the darkness. The house leans away from prevailing winds. Weeds grow high and tangled around it.

When the new cotton crop came in, the oil mill started up and we moved back to Jayton, in good time for me to start in the second grade. Nannie Beth Rice was my teacher. She's in the Jayton cemetery now, dead in 1950 at age 43. I wish you hadn't done that, Nannie Beth. I wish I knew who you were. She's buried in the Rice family plot with her father (d. 1933) and her mother, Lula Knudson Rice (d. 1962), and a sister, Callie Janet Rice (1904–1917), that I didn't know about, but on the tombstone her name is Nannie Beth Brown. Who was he, Nannie Beth, and who are you, and why are you here, and how did you come home again?

We moved into the sixth house I remember, the house I think of most often when I think of Jayton, the little house on the Lowrance place, their big house and our little house the northernmost dwellings in Jayton, ours not ten yards from a drop-off into the Croton Breaks. I remember the house, though it is gone: I remember leaving my new ball and glove on the porch overnight and the dog mangling them just a bit; I remember going with my mother and father and brother into the Breaks to chop down a Christmas tree to bring home; I remember my mother's making three pies at a time and cutting each into fourths so that a pie disappeared each meal. I remember when Grandpa died and they brought him in his coffin to our house to be there for family and friends; I remember being pleased with the importance of the occasion and scared out of my mind. I remember hours, hours, hours in the Croton Breaks, right out the back door. Later, for some years, the house was used for hay storage, but then a few years ago they tore it down, and it is gone.

Then we moved into the seventh house, uptown, into the east half of the Callicoate house, while I was in the third grade. Miss Sue Kinney was my teacher, fresh from her degree at what is now Sul Ross State University, and I was deeply in love with her and much mortified when, after I saw an episode or two of "The Mark of Zorro," the Saturday serial, she singled me out for minor punishment for drawing pictures of Zorro and distributing them. We weren't in that house long, but that Christmas I did come to own my first book, and those were the only electric lights I knew until later. The house is still there and seems in good repair, but is not the house I knew.

When did I spend time at the farm with Grandma and Grandpa? Was it one summer? Two summers? Every summer? Have I converted the memory of one dear time into memory of habitual experiences? We humans often do. When did I spend time there? Have all the fresh corn I could eat? Play Chinese checkers with Grandma, dominoes with Grandpa? Roam the farm? Walk across the railroad trestle and run down the bank at one end to see how far momentum would get me up the bank at the other? When did I have the one magical train ride of my youth, from Gilpin, the post office/grocery store/service station down the way from the farm, all the way home to Jayton? I don't know.

The eighth house I remember living in was our last house in Jayton, just off the street that turned from the old main street toward the school, alongside the Sproules' place. It was a good house, twelve dollars a month rent, four whole rooms with a good outhouse and our first radio, though we were back to coal oil lamps. In the unused pas-

ture across the dirt road, three or four of us dug a cave and roofed it with scrap tin and lumber, and sat in the darkness and told stories, but not of the deaths of kings, for we knew none. The house is still there. I saw it that Saturday in 1986, not faring badly, though it looks deserted.

After that, it was mostly the big city.

By then, you see, it was late 1939. I had come to the fourth grade. Mrs. Check Jay was my teacher, wife to one of the family for whom the town was named. The weather was no better, rainfall no greater, the cotton worse, and the oil mill shut down. When my father finally found work there, we moved to Fort Worth, and were gone from Jayton for good.

I was lonesome before, looking out across the Croton Breaks, wondering what I was looking for, looking way across town toward the Double Mountains, blue in the distance, wondering what I was looking for, not knowing, and I have been more lonesome since.

But why the hell would it matter?

Why would it matter?

We were there only about five years. We were transients. No one noticed that we were there, or remembered. How did those five years come to matter so? What was I looking for?

I have half-joked when people have inquired why I stayed at my job in Fort Worth, have told them there were three reasons: that it was an unnecessary cost of spirit and energy to move, that I could see the western horizon from my front porch, that I could get to West Texas quickly if I needed to. Why, I wonder, did I think I might need to, after all those years? What did I expect to look for, and maybe find? Am I, have I been, a transient even while still? Has my life been a mistake, waiting somehow for West Texas? What was I hoping to see? Was I waiting all that time for something that wasn't there? Or wasn't there for me? What was I waiting to know?

—— 9 ——
Interlude: Where Are You, Jimmy?

But wait. Not so fast. Hold everything. Something else happened. I hadn't intended to, but I went back to Jayton. I had resolved not to go back, but went anyway, on June 25, 1987, went back on a single mission, to read verses and memorial lines on tombstones for another little project I was working on as time allowed. I had little time, didn't allow myself time, didn't want to take time, wanted to get to the cemetery, copy lines and verses (God knows why, I hope) and get back to work.

But in the meantime, I'd been reading the *Chronicle*, learning again or for the first time about events, seeing the names of people. Since I was going to be there anyway, I thought I'd stop in and ask Cornelia Cheyne at the courthouse about them, and I did. I asked her about Jimmy Matthews, my best friend, and about the Jones family, especially Don, also my best friend, and about the Robinson family, especially sweet Peggy Sue, and about Bobbie Nell Fuller and Tom Wade. I asked about Whatley and Hancock and Brown and Cox. I asked how Nannie Beth Rice came to be Nannie Beth Brown and why she died at 43 and why she's in the cemetery without her husband.

I believe Cornelia remembered Nannie Beth, but didn't know that she was dead, or buried in the Jayton cemetery.

She didn't know—and why would she?—why the American Legion post was named for Whatley and Hancock, not for Cox and Brown, not for all four. She wondered if maybe Cox and Brown had moved away from Jayton before going into the service.

She remembered Tom Wade, but didn't know where he is, or whether he's alive. Tom was my brother's best friend and the son of Mr. Wade, the owner and editor of the *Jayton Chronicle*. For a while maybe, in the late 1950s and the early 1960s, Tom came back and ran the *Chronicle* after Mr. Wade's death, but she didn't know what had become of him.

She didn't remember Peggy Sue. When I asked about the Bake Robinson family, she thought I was talking about Bake Jr., Peggy Sue's older brother, not Red, the other one, not Mr. Bake Robinson, and thought maybe they were in New Mexico.

She didn't remember Don Jones, or which branch of the Jones family he belonged to.

But when I asked about Bobbie Nell Fuller, a strange thing happened. I asked about Bobbie Nell because in my memory she was the blond princess of our class (though my heart belonged to Peggy Sue), and because I had seen a front-page story about her wedding in the *Chronicle*. The wedding took place before she would have finished high school. "Why, yes, I know Bobbie Nell, have all along," Mrs. Cheyne said. "She lives over yonder." She pointed to a pleasant house at the southwest corner of the square, just one house and a dirt street from the abandoned office of the *Jayton Chronicle*. "She never left, far's I know."

And when I asked about Jimmy Matthews, a strange thing happened. "Oh, yes," she said. "I know Jimmy. He moved back last year. I don't know where he'd been. He bought a farm somewhere here outside of town, but he lives in the rock house across from the Church of Christ. You can't miss it."

I went by and looked and was glad of the house, but didn't stop. I didn't try to talk to either of them.

I've wondered why I didn't. I know some of the reasons, but not all, not all. Perhaps the words about Jayton inside my own head had become more real than the people and places and events they tried to name. Bobbie Nell's version and Jimmy's version might be too different from my own. They might startle me into believing that I had Jayton all wrong, and if I had Jayton all wrong, what else did I get wrong? Perhaps, that day, I just wanted more time to think through my version.

I could have stopped to see them, could have said, "How was life, Jimmy? How did you see it? Where were you when you looked? Have I told any of the truth? Will I know any of it when I finish reading the *Jayton Chronicle*?"

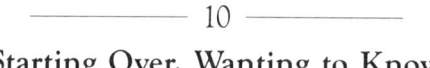

10

Starting Over, Wanting to Know

I thought it would be, not simple perhaps, but simpler than it turned out to be. I would find the *Jayton Chronicle* and measure life in the

Chronicle against life in my memory. I'd see then what news I learned, and catch surprises, news I thought I already had, but had wrong, would learn how far that world might be, and maybe learn why it seemed so far.

Seemed a simple enough project, mostly straightforward, a matter of checking this against that. Seemed simple enough, though not simple. Wasn't. Didn't work out that way. There was too much to think about and to try to remember, myself least but omnipresent, except in the pages of the *Chronicle*.

However I lived in those years, I lived without seeing some things. I want to think that I saw some things—the Double Mountains, say, or the Croton Breaks, very well, but now I've come to know that I simply didn't see much of life in Jayton. Perhaps I don't, after all, have to blame myself for not seeing. I was a kid, not yet real. But I should have looked, taken notice. Perhaps that's why I came finally to read the *Chronicle*. I wanted to know how it was then. I want to know how it is now. I want to know how now is different from then. I want to know how I got from one to the other.

How can I catch those years? Much of my own recent time is gone and irretrievable. When I look at my *curriculum vitae*, the report of life sacred to academics, years are missing, and I cannot catch them, those years I cannot get straight. I think I have all the publications recorded—they are in print, anyway, and could be found, should I remember to look and remember also where to look. My principal job—the one I get paid a regular salary for—is a matter of record. What I have lost, what is unrecorded and irretrievable, is whatever else I did professionally for some years—I'm leaving events of my personal life out of account. I begin to understand that I've often lived without seeing, not just when I was a baby, and, not seeing, cannot now remember or record.

For maybe ten years, I was reasonably active in a public though minor sort of way. For a while there, wherever three people, myself included, were gathered together, I made a speech or presented a paper or conducted a workshop. I spoke to student groups, to high school teachers, to college teachers, to administrators, probably to passing strangers. I wrote for the student newspaper on the campus where I teach, and for the student magazine, and for the alumni magazine. In some months of some of those years, these extra chores came frequently, sometimes three or four or five special events in a month. But I kept no record, have no file, or list of dates or organizations or events. I told myself during those years that doing such things was part of my job, that I deserved no congratulations or notice on my record, that the work was standard, that it was what I did to keep from being thrown in jail. And so I kept no record.

Now those events are gone. I know that I was in Lafayette, Indiana, doing something, and in Wichita Falls, Texas, and in Uvalde and Comanche and Stephenville and Orange and Kingsville and in Providence, Rhode Island; and in Dallas and Abilene and Bossier City, and in Chicago and Indianapolis; and somewhere told members of the Texas Poetry Society that they had been following wrong gods for most of the twentieth century; and I don't know where else, and can't trust my memory to tell me where or when or why or to whom I spoke. I have no record and can't catch my own recent past. I look for what remains, and I look, too, for what has vanished. How can I catch those years in the *Jayton Chronicle*? I can't even catch my own recent years.

Sometimes, I like to start my freshman composition class in the fall with some propositions for writers. I want, I think, to shy away from the conventional advice of composition textbooks, which is mostly not too useful. These propositions—all, I like to think, wonderfully dramatized with anecdotes, analyses, games, and discussions—are mostly plain. "You have to get situated to see," I tell them, meanwhile trying to demonstrate with my little games that they are not necessarily so situated. "What you see ought to be what you need to see," I tell them, meanwhile trying to show them that they have not necessarily seen what they need to see. "Once you're situated to see," I tell them, "and once you've looked at what you think you need to see," I tell them, "then try to show me what you've seen so that I can see it, too."

Not bad advice, if it's made real and immediate. The trouble is, I can't always follow it myself, can't get situated to see, can't see what I must, can't tell another what I think I've seen. I've looked and tried, looked for myself, for others, but I can't get the job done.

A stranger to the ground, I've stood at the place marked with an x on the map to tell me where Bowie died, have told myself, "This is the place where it happened." Were the thick walls damp that March, I've wondered, or did dust puff by their feet as they passed from the chapel, by the wall, along the wall to the place where Bowie died? Dying is tedious work, I've thought, and lonesome. It would not have been hot yet, that March. Did he sweat cold from fever? Dying is dirty, hard work. When he heard the *dequella*, did it tell him more about death than I can know? Did he know that this is the place where it happened?

Was Crockett his friend? His room was small. When the world came scuffling in, did he know, or stand upon his x, as I do?

"This is the place where it happened," I've told myself. I guess it was harried work, and grating, dying that March. Maps are more certain than I've been, only sensing somewhere a sudden scuffle in a lonesome room when he died that March. I wish I could know I had the x right marking the place where it happened, but oh, it is hard work any March, to know Bowie and all your x's.

I can't get situated to see, can't see what I must, can't tell another what I think I've seen. That doesn't stay me against the presumption that I sometimes know, know that the what they know of me is not the what I know, know that what I was is not what I am, what I am not what I was, what I was not what I was, what I am not what I am. What I am floats in someone's perception, maybe here, maybe there, and I can't with sureness testify to my own existence. Won't. Don't know how. Might. Better not. Can't.

My testimony, after all, I'd base on chancy knowledge, faulty memory. Is that the way with testimony? Much that I saw, I saw wrong or misunderstood, or measured only against myself.

But not just wrong: right, one way or another, one time or another. Time, history, our lives—all are palimpsests. We write or talk and know, then erase and do it again, and scrape it all away and do it again, and revise and do it all again, and each version is wrong—and right. I thought I had my mother clear in my mind, but didn't.

A hymn had been running through my mind all day, and I had been singing it while I worked in the office, except for the one word that I couldn't remember. I don't know that the people in nearby offices entirely appreciated my singing, but no matter, I sang, except for the one word:

> When the trumpet of the Lord shall sound,
> And time shall be no more,
> When the morning breaks eternal bright and fair,
> When the HUM of earth shall gather over on the other shore,
> And the roll is called up yonder, I'll be there.

And then the refrain:

> When the ROLL is called up yonder,
> When the ROLL is called up yonder,
> When the ROLLL is called up yonder,
> When the roll is called up yonder, I'll be there.

When I got home that night, I called my parents for the word. Actually, I called my mother. Some things you can call her about; other things you have to call my father about.

When she came to the phone, I said, "I need to know a word in a hymn."

She said, "Why?"

I said, "Because."

She said, "Well, what is it?"

I said, "If I knew what it was, I wouldn't call you."

She said, "I meant the hymn, the hymn."

I told her I didn't know the title, but could sing it except for one word, which I did:

> When the trumpet of the Lord shall sound,
> And time shall be no more,
> And the morning breaks eternal bright and fair,
> When the HUM of earth shall gather over on the other shore,
> And the roll is called up yonder, I'll be there.

"I need to know what goes in place of HUM," I told her, "you know, 'When the HUM of earth shall gather over on the other shore.'"

"Well," she said, "let me think." Then I heard her humming and singing:

> When the HUM HUM of the HUM shall HUM,
> And HUM shall be no HUM,
> And the HUM HUM breaks eternal HUM and HUM,
> When the SAVED of earth shall gather over on the other shore,
> And the roll is call up yonder, I'll be there.

"It's *saved*," she said, and I was about to thank her, but she wasn't through:

> When the ROLL is called up yonder,
> When the ROLL is called up yonder,
> When the ROLLL is called up yonder,
> When the roll is called up yonder, I'll be there.

We talked a minute, and I thanked her and told her goodbye before she got to wondering whether I was among the "saved" that she had remembered for me.

I called again not too long after that. Part of another hymn was catching in my mind, and I'd been singing at the office again. I'd not want you to think that it's always hymns I sing. I sing television advertising jingles a lot, and I particularly favor "I Didn't Know God Made Honky Tonk Angels," but this time it was another hymn. I could only

remember and sing one line: "Here I raise mine ebenezer." I didn't especially want to know all of the rest of the words, but I was curious about
the title.

As it happens, that hymn caused me considerable puzzlement
when I was a boy and we'd sing it in church. I always wondered what
an "ebenezer" was. It sounded sort of like a hat since the song said,
"Here I raise mine ebenezer," and I always intended to ask my parents
about it when we got home from church, but I always forgot. Not too
long ago I remembered to look it up myself, and discovered that an
ebenezer was a memorial stone referred to in 1 Samuel 7:12. But that
wasn't the point of my calling this time—I just wanted to know the name
of the hymn, for no particular reason except that the melody and that
one line had been in my mind.

My father answered the phone, and we talked a minute or two,
and then I told him I needed to talk to my mother about a hymn. I'd
not be able to explain why if my life depended on it, I suppose, but
I had long ago decided that there were some things you asked my father about and there were other things you asked my mother about.

When she came to the phone, I told her I needed to know about
another hymn.

"You writing a book about hymns?" she said. "I thought you promised you'd write a western." My mother likes western novels.

"No, I'm not writing a book. I was just curious," I told her.

"Well, what is it?" she said.

"I don't know. That's why I called you."

"Well, do I have to guess, or do you remember anything about it?"

Then I told her that I only remembered one line, and I sang it
for her: "Here I raise mine ebenezer." I told her I wanted to know what
the title was. "Well," she said, "let me think a minute." She began half
singing, half humming:

> Here I HUM mine HUM HUM HUM HUM
> HUM HUM HUM HUM, HUM HUM HUM . . .

By now I was hearing noise in the background. Turned out it was my
father, asking what I wanted to know. I heard her tell him about the
ebenezer line, and then she went on singing and humming. After a
minute or so I heard more noise in the background. He was singing
and humming, too, and my mother said, "You'll have to wait. He's singing, too, and you know how he sings. I can't keep the tune with that
noise." I did indeed know how he sings and how he raised a joyful noise

to the Lord on Sunday mornings. "When I think of it," my mother said, "I'll call you."

In about five minutes the phone rang, and I answered it. "It's 'Come Thou Fount,'" she said, and then she sang it, ebenezer and all. After a while, I thanked her, and we said goodbyes.

Other things, I'd ask my father about. Family things, old times—for these I go to him. Well, not always, I guess, but sometimes. It's interesting what memory holds and doesn't hold. I remember the serial number of my rifle from army times, 1950 to 1952, but of course sometimes do not remember the papers I was supposed to bring to school with me this morning. I sometimes remember who was in movies in the early 1940s, but forget where I left off in class yesterday. These peculiarities may be owing to a general and advancing decrepitude, not quite yet become senility. I think not. I hope not.

But I was talking about memory. When I go looking for something that simply isn't in my memory, I think I'm usually glad enough to accept what somebody else—say my father—will supply. Not long ago I was trying to remember how we kept milk in the old days, but had no fragment or signal in my mind. I called my father.

"Did we have an ice box all of the time when we lived in Jayton?" I asked him. "I don't remember using one all of the time."

I could hear him waiting, thinking. "Yes," he finally said, "yes, we did."

"I don't remember using one all of the time," I said again.

"Well," he said, "we had an ice box all of the time, but we didn't always have enough money for ice."

"Well," I asked, how did we keep milk?"

"Well," he said, "when we didn't have ice, we either kept the milk in the cow, or we didn't keep it."

That seemed to settle that.

I called him another time because I didn't know what they called those things at the mill where he worked—they were wheeled hand vehicles, but they weren't wheelbarrows. They were designed to carry six one-hunded-pound sacks of cattle feed. "What did you call those things at the mill," I asked when he answered the phone, "that the men used to move six one-hundred-pound bags?"

"Hand trucks," he said, and that settled that.

I'd been thinking about them for no particular reason. Images of the men with those hand trucks had been flitting in my mind, and I'd simply been trying to get the names of things straight. The feed was made in the upwards of the mill and poured, one hundred pounds each time, into open checkerboard sacks on a conveyor belt on the main floor. The filled and open sacks moved then along the belt to the sewing machine near the big wide door, where Long John neatly sewed them and neatly flipped them out of his way. The young men's job was to load six on each hand truck and wheel the loads out the door, down the loading dock, across a metal ramp, and into the box cars that were waiting on the line that went right alongside the mill.

I remember watching the young men with great wonder. I would have been maybe twelve or thirteen or fourteen. When one of them would get six one-hundred-pound sacks stacked on his hand truck, he'd make a slight, graceful leap up on the handles, using his weight, gravity, and the leverage supplied by the design of the hand truck to get the handles down into pushing position. Then he'd move quickly to the big door, leap lightly again, this time with his weight on one handle, and turn the hand truck at right angle down the loading dock. The thing to do then, apparently, was to build as much momentum as possible for the last graceful leaps that would turn the truck at right angle off the loading dock onto the metal ramp and into the box car and then at right angle again inside the box car, to stop suddenly with the six sacks stacked neatly alongside the stacks already there.

They were hand trucks. I had just wanted to know the name that went with those leaps that were so quick and graceful for me to see, though days of such work must finally have had a killing toll to take of those young men. I didn't know that then. I knew that they were graceful and strong.

Mostly, I guess, if something isn't in my memory and somebody—say my mother or my father or my Uncle Elmer, but not necessarily Cousin Duane—fills the vacancy, I am usually glad enough to take and trust. It startles me, though, when I discover that what I thought I had fixed clearly in my memory turns out to be unlike the truth, or maybe like only the tiniest portion of the truth, or maybe like what was true once, but never more.

Not long ago I found myself singing another hymn that had a hole in it, a single word I couldn't get. I knew the name of the hymn. It was "On Jordan's Stormy Banks," and it goes like this:

> On Jordan's stormy banks I stand
> And cast a wistful eye,
> Where Canaan's fair and happy land
> And my HUM HUM HUM HUM lie.

And then the refrain:

> I am bound for the Promised LAAAnnd,
> I am bound for the Promised Land.
> O who will come and go with me?
> I am bound for the Promised Land.

At Sunday night services a long time ago, sometimes the preacher wouldn't preach. Instead, we'd just sing hymns, and the preacher would call for requests. I thought then that this was something you were supposed to do every once in a while in church. It didn't occur to me until many cynical years later that maybe we did it because the preacher didn't have it in him some Sundays to prepare two sermons. Mr. Jimmy Johnston with a *T* (I thought all of that was his name) always requested "On Jordan's Stormy Banks," except he said Jerdan. I asked my parents why he said it that way and they said, "Just because." One day I chanced to mention the matter at the dinner table and my daughter said, "Well, Daddy, sometimes people from particular regions of the country elevate the point of articulation for vowels, so Jordan becomes Jerdan." I think that's the same as "just because," but longer.

Anyway, I couldn't remember one word in the fourth line of the first verse. From the rhythm, I was pretty sure it was a four-syllable word.

I called my mother. I told her I had lost a word from another hymn and asked her if she would kindly provide it. "What goes in the blank space?" I asked her, and sang:

> On Jordan's stormy banks I stand
> And cast a wistful eye,
> Where Canaan's fair and happy land
> And my HUM HUM HUM HUM lie.

She was quiet for a moment. Then I heard her singing and humming:

> On Jordan's HUM HUM banks I HUM
> And cast a HUM HUM eye,
> Where Canaan's HUM and happy land
> And my—

"It's *possessions*," she said:

> Where Canaan's fair and happy land
> And my possessions lie.

When she sang it, I understood why I thought it was four syllables:

> Where Canaan's fair and happy land
> And my po-o-sess-ions lie.

Okay, I thought. It's "possessions." But then it came upon me that this didn't sound right. My mother was still on the phone. "But if they're across the river and you've never been there," I asked her, "how can they be your *possessions?*"

Nothing for a moment. Then she said, very patiently, "Well, according to the doctrine of grace, what lies there waiting *is* yours, even if you haven't been there before. Didn't you pay attention at church?"

"Oh," I said, "I see."

After a moment or two we said goodbye.

I gnawed for a while on what she'd said. This, I told myself, is very strange. Not the grace part—I understood what she meant. What I didn't understand was her saying it at all. This wasn't the mother I had fixed clearly in my mind through all the years. I wasn't surprised that she knew about grace—she may have invented it, for all I know. What surprised me was the careful, instructive enunciation of the principle. She didn't say things like that before, I thought, not in that way. Had she had the audacity, I wondered, to have grown and learned and changed all the time that I thought *I* was the one growing and learning and changing?

After I thought about it a little while, I decided that yes, I guess she had had the audacity to do just that. I thought I had her right once, and didn't. I may have her right now, but won't swear to it.

11

Looking for What's Gone

"It takes time to be touched by things," Charlie Smith says in one of his poems, "sometimes it takes time." Then he goes on:

> I admit that some truth
> is immediate, like: 'America is a large country'
> or 'big, bouncy breasts'
> or 'Charleston, South Carolina,'
> but usually I have been off in the south pasture

for days digging out stumps
when whatever it was I should have gotten
nabs me. Once, when I was four, Hopalong Cassidy
visited my town on his white horse
and I missed him. Years later I was going to become a Buddhist,
but I started thinking about Hopalong Cassidy, that
black suit, those silky guns,
that white horse; I wondered
what Hoppy would think of my becoming a Buddhist
and I hemmed and hawed
until the opportunity skipped away. That's what I mean,
nearly exactly,
about the delay of being touched. It's like the day
my brother said. 'My time is almost up.'
and I went on dredging out the well,
as if clearing a circle of water in back of the house
were the most important thing in the world,
and didn't listen.

I should have paid attention, should have known you then, Mother, and now. Now I look for you in the *Jayton Chronicle*, and for others, and for myself, but I don't find us. I see my name, Jimmie Wayne Corder, once in a while in *Chronicle* reports in 1937 and 1938 of the honor roll up at the school, but that's scarcely myself, though I was there. I read accounts of Jimmy Matthews in football games in the fall, 1945, and again in the fall, 1946, when I surely wasn't there, and think, "I should have been there with you, Jimmy—together we'd have been better than all right, together we'd have pulled it off." Who were they, those people I read about?

In a joint review of books about and by Beryl Markham and about Bror Blixen, Diane Ackerman remarks:

> Biographies seem doomed to fail. If even corsages lose their color pressed between the pages, what hope has a life? Lying in state, in print, a life can look formal, orderly and planned. But suppose the life were in many ways a mess, albeit a fascinating, courageous, picturesque and emotionally intense mess?
>
> Beryl Markham lived such a life, about which she and others often lied. Along with those colorful figures T. E. Lawrence and Sir Richard Burton, Markham was one of the most extraordinary of explorers. That a life of high public drama, scandal, eccentricity, and passion could be lost for so long, only to be rediscovered by accident, makes you wonder how many other electrifying stories have disappeared into the guidelines of history.

Why would she wonder, I wonder? Don't we already know that most are lost? Electrifying lives—not necessarily lives "of high public drama" —are gone. I look for what remains, and cannot find it, and I look for what is gone, and cannot find it. "How was life, Jimmy? How did you see it? Where were you when you looked? Have I told any of the truth? Will I know any of it when I finish reading the *Jayton Chronicle?*"

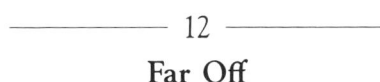

12

Far Off

Sometimes, when I hear a child's call, say far down the block past the arching green trees, or maybe way over on the next street and down, or maybe just at twilight, I want to go and be her guard, or his, and teach the child safely home. Sometimes a child calls, far off, maybe just at twilight. Sometimes, I know who the child is and where home is, and want to hold her safe, or him.

13

Fall Always Comes

Fall always comes. Any season, I know, can be melancholy, for all seasons send us down toward death. Fall is woeful enough for me, though there's reason to think otherwise.

I remember standing on the rim of the canyons, late afternoons, looking as far as I could see and being suddenly lonesome—for what, I couldn't have said at the time or maybe now—maybe already lonesome for all that I would lose or never gain, for all that I would never say, see, hear, or be.

Still, there have always been reasons for thinking fall a happy season. It offers rest from the heat and drought that are ours in the summer here on the edge of the Great American Desert. It brings the new year. I've been in school one way or another for fifty years. When that is the circumstance, you come to know that January 1 is a minor holiday. The new year actually commences some time around September 1. Things begin then. Things left off for the summer are picked up again. If you are a school teacher, as I am, you even get to believe that the first day of school is Resurrection Day, and this time around you'll do better. Sometimes that feeling lasts a while. Sometimes it doesn't.

When fall comes and the time is right, there is a moon beyond magic to see. They say that when the harvest moon is full and you see it large and low in the east—if you're not surrounded by all the things we've built to block our vision—they say, I was about to mention, that you can restore the harvest moon to its proper proportion by turning your back on it and then bending over to look at it between your legs. I never tried that. I don't know why anyone would want to.

Fall brings a moon beyond magic, and blue northers. To me, on the small side of eternity, the blue norther may be the most exhilarating event it's possible to know. On the day a blue norther comes, the wind will be blowing maybe pretty gently, most likely from the south or southwest. Then, when you're not paying attention, the wind will stop, and the air will be still except for an occasional twist to swirl the leaves for a moment. If you have been paying attention, you will have seen by this time in the north and northwest a blue line of clouds. If you are familiar with blue northers, that time of stillness is high with expectation.

Then, bye and bye, it comes, sometimes with rain or sleet, often dry because it whistles in and through so fast that it doesn't have time to rain. It will take your breath for a moment if it's a good one, maybe dropping the temperature fifty degrees in an afternoon. If you're out in the open when the blue norther comes down, and if you face into it and give yourself to it, for a moment or two you'll get a quick glimpse of a notion about what it feels like to be the Lord God Almighty riding the wind down along the slopes of the Rockies, across the Panhandle, down off the Cap Rock, and home.

That ought to be enough to make the fall a sweet time. It isn't. I'm not young any more. I seldom go out and give myself to northers any more. The harvest is past, the summer is ended, and I am not saved.

I have waited on the promises of picking time and have once in a while seen the fulfillment of promises. But even when I was young and stood on the rim of the canyons looking into the blue distance, an autumnal chill sometimes shivered my bones and wrapped around me like a winding sheet. Since, even in happy Septembers and radiant Octobers, that chill has cut deeper and deeper. Somewhere along the way I learned to expect grief. I have heard a child's call far off. I will be sad come fall, and I think there's scant hope for consolation. If fall can be a sweet, high time, fresh with new beginnings, it is also a leaving time, a parting time, a dying time. We're all, I suppose, sometimes afraid that it's all going away, as we dread that we are dying, as we always are.

I know that not everyone is as cowardly as I, as timorous and fearful, as accustomed to expecting grief. But surely somewhere out there sits someone who lives as I do, waiting, like the Comanches in Palo Duro Canyon. To be sure, they had gone to the Red River and danced with the Kiowas, following Ishatai into a last great Sun Dance to nerve themselves up, as we sometimes do, but then, not much later, they found themselves in Palo Duro Canyon, waiting, and when they looked up, the future came down upon them with Mackenzie's troopers. Then the world was over for the Comanches, though none died on the spot. They found the loneliness that we wait for.

Against the loneliness I have no stay. Against the loneliness I have stored no treasures. I have only quick images to cheer me, and dear memories; I haven't held on to history, or got history told right to linger over. I have made no films, kept no scrapbooks, and such photographs as I have are scattered. I can't get the past to stay with me. If I could, I'd have it wrong. When fall comes and the fallen leaves skitter before a twist of wind, I'll be sad. The past disappears out from under me, and one day it will catch me and I will disappear, too. I have waited for grief, and never knew that when it came, it would look very much like myself. I will be sad come fall, and do not expect consolation. The harvest is past, the summer is ended, and I am not saved.

The Palo Duro Canyon happens, I know, for most of us, if not all; every season takes us toward death, and "each country," Zulfikar Ghose says, "is an Israel for someone." Our words beat against memory, against the knowledge that people and places and things are not in an eternal present. We discover that this is so, and then ache that it is. We're always falling into history; every word we utter both finds and loses ourselves, our pasts, our places. In the past ten years or so, many have cried for a lost authority and called it back, not least, most recently, that strange Trinity—Secretary of Education Bennett, Allan Bloom, and E. D. Hirsch, the last of whom now wants to standardize us all to a past of his foundation's making.

We all seem slow to know that when we come into history, we lose authority and location. We are not in the eternal present: things die, and things change. Each person, whether or not aware, is all of history, and each, by saying words, falls, and falls, and falls again, re-enacting falls. "History is often compared to a woven fabric," Octavio Paz says, "the work of many hands; without deciding on a pattern beforehand, and without knowing exactly what they are doing, these hands weave threads of every color together until a succession of figures, at once familiar and enigmatic, appears on the loom. From the point of view of 'short duration' the figures are not repeated; history is constant creation, novelty, the realm of the unique and singular. From the standpoint of 'long duration,' repetitions, ruptures, and renewals can be perceived; rhythms. Both visions are true." We fall, and fall again, even when we are solitary.

The understanding of "long duration," Paz says, "gives us the feeling that we are before a historical landscape—that is to say, before a history that exhibits the immobility of nature. A misleading impression: nature also moves and changes. The changes of 'short duration' register on this apparently immobile background like phenomena that alter the physiognomy of the place: the coming and going of light and darkness, noon and twilight, rain and storms, the wind that blows the clouds before it and raises whirls of dust." Over yonder, we make a small diaspora. Down there we timidly join the Comanches in Palo Duro Canyon. Over here, we change the traditional for the modern and recapitulate the Industrial Revolution as each generation grows old. Pope always has to keep writing *The Dunciad*, for we are still destroying an older society, still emerging in a world we inhabit but do not know. We make a little holocaust, and find the world come round again, as Fred Chappell shows in his poem, "Skin Flick":

> The selfsame surface that billowed once with
> the shapes of Trigger and Jane. New faces now
> Are in the saddle. Tits and buttocks
> Slide rattling down the beam as down
> A coal chute; in the splotched light
> the burning bush strikes dumb.
>
> Different sort of cattle drive:
> No water for miles and miles.
>
> In the aisles, new bugs and rats
> Though it's the same Old Paint.
>
> Audience of lepers, hopeless and homeless,
> Or like the buffalo, at home
> In the wind only. No
> Mushy love stuff for them.

They eye the violent innocence they always knew.
Is that the rancher's palomino daughter?
Is this her eastern finishing school?

Same old predicament:
No water for miles and miles,
The horizon breeds no cavalry.

Men draw your wagons in a circle. Be ready.

I guess I wanted Jayton in the *Chronicle* to be some Eden, and it was not. I see my name once in a while in *Chronicle* reports in 1937 and 1938 of the honor roll up at the school, but that's scarcely myself, though I was there.

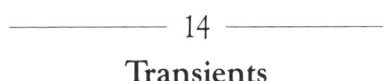

14

Transients

Once, that spring of 1937, I stayed home from school sick, and a hard, dark dust storm blew in, though the sun was still there above. That afternoon, when my brother got off the bus and started home, the dust was blowing so hard that he lost his way and had to backtrack to find home. Later, he swore to me that the sun was shining above the dust and the dust was thick, and he saw his shadow in the air beside him, and I believed him, and I still do. But even if I have it all wrong, brother, we were not shadows in the air, not shadows, brother, not shadows.

15

Seeing and Not Seeing

I have half-joked when people have inquired why I stayed at my job in Fort Worth all these years, have told them there were three reasons: that it was an unnecessary cost of spirit and energy to move, that I could see the western horizon from my front porch, that I could get to West Texas quickly if I needed to. Perhaps I thought—perhaps I still think—that one day I'll really learn about the Great Depression of the 1930s, even if I have to look at it through my own, that one day I'll really know what that Dust Bowl drought was like. Perhaps, latterly, I began to catch on that what I'd seen was worth seeing, if only I could see it right—World War II and all that followed, so much and so quickly. Perhaps I thought that one day I'd really know that country, that history.

But it turned out to be so far. Knowledge is chancy. Evidence disappears. The other issues of the *Chronicle* are gone. The issues I have are told in their own way, not in the way anyone else would tell. Memory always fails. My interpretation of events is unilateral, but the world isn't. I wanted to find and to know people, events, places. I have studied maps, looking for myself, but I'm not there.

What I saw, I often saw wrong, then misremembered. Most things I didn't see at all and now can't find.

For all these years I have treasured my first train ride—and my only train ride until I was on past thirty and then rode clear up to Chicago for a meeting and back. I have treasured that first and only train ride, kept it in my mind, glad it was there, have taken it out from time to time and turned it this way and that, felt of it, have told my children about it too often, have sometimes troubled innocent passers with the story.

I think it must have been in the summer of 1938. Might have been 1937, but I think not—we lived part of that summer just two or three miles away while my father worked for the Highway Department, before we moved back to Jayton and I started the second grade. It was the summer of 1938. My parents had taken me to stay on the farm with Grandma and Grandpa—a week, maybe more, I don't know. When it was time to go home, I got to ride the train. Grandma cooked tea cakes and filled a sack for me to take. Then Grandpa and I walked down to Gilpin, maybe close to a mile away down the railroad track. Gilpin was a one-building mark on the map, a post office, service station, and grocery. The man at Gilpin put out a flag to tell the train to stop. The train left Stamford every morning, went up through Aspermont, Swenson, Jayton, and Girard to Spur, then came back in the afternoon. That time it stopped for me at Gilpin and I rode home in glory, seated on leather in the caboose, smelling smoke and wood, amazed by the black coat and the stiff white collar of the conductor, who talked to me, though I was mostly afraid to answer.

I have remembered that as my first and only train ride until after I was thirty, have remembered the leather and smoke and polished wood, the stiff white collar, my sack of tea cakes, and I have told the story too often.

I did ride the train that time, but it wasn't my first or only ride. The *Chronicle* shows otherwise.

Under "School News" the *Chronicle* for Thursday, October 21, 1937, shows that I took another, earlier, train ride *and wrote about it.* In his introduction, Mr. Wade says that the ride occurred "last Tuesday," which might be October 19 or October 12. Then this follows:

> This story is about our train ride. We rode the train from Jayton to Girard. The first grade went with us. We rode back on the bus. We had a good time. We waited for the train at the depot. Then the train came and we were off. It was very crowded.
>
> I saw cotton fields and cows and horses. We sang going up there and we sang coming back. We all rode on one big ticket. Miss Rice bought it.
>
> —Jimmie Wayne Corder

What I saw, I often saw wrong, and then misremembered. Most, I didn't see at all.

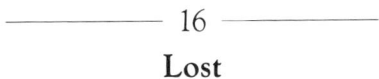

16

Lost

I don't want to be constructed or interpreted. I want to be known and acknowledged. I want not to be invisible.

When I ask my students in freshman English to write essays, I write the assignment too, and turn my work over to them when they turn their essays in to me. I don't know that anyone gains much by this practice. I do know that it creates grave problems for me when I grade their papers. When I give them copies of the essays I have written, I don't want them to grade me. I want them to listen to me, to pay attention, to notice how clever I've been in the third paragraph, how astute and perceptive on page four. Then I come to imagine that they may once in a while feel that way when they give their papers to me: "Don't grade me—listen, pay attention, notice that I'm here."

Much that I see, I see wrong, and then misremember, my first misinterpretation veering ever wider of the mark. I try to justify myself: I didn't always know the signifiers, *couldn't* always know them. My parents kept me from knowing how they pawned my father's watch. I wasn't old enough or observant enough to know about the vicissitudes of theater ownership in Jayton. I didn't know until long after I was grown

that Grandpa Durham—that stern and righteous Baptist—sometimes made persimmon beer and cooled it in the cistern.

But even now, when I hunt and look and sometimes see, I can't catch it all. Artifacts tell a lot, but not everything. Try as I will, try as you will, we can't catch and map the place where others invent their worlds.

Some years ago, my wife's aunt came by and left us a multicolored burlap bag full of matchbooks. They'd been collecting them for years. "They're no good to us any more," she said. "The kids are gone, and nobody looks at them. They're just taking up space. Your kids might like to look at them."

In the bag there were—I don't know—maybe a thousand match-books, and they came from all over—the Stagecoach Inn at Salado, Lau Yee Chi at Waikiki, the Swiss Chalet in Rochelle Park, New Jersey, and Mitchell's Premium Beer. We spilled them out from time to time and looked, and there was the Sand and Sage in Denver, the Jack Tar Motel in Galveston, and W&W Pickles from Montgomery, Alabama. Mostly, though, I smoked them up. Their hobby, you see, didn't turn out to be mine. The fun, I guess, is in the finding, not in the having.

Sometimes when I would rummage around in the bag hunting for matches, I would sit and look and try to understand how they were, the aunt and uncle, and their two sons. I would sit and wonder where they were when they found each book, and wonder what they were like. Were all four of them interested in the matchbooks, I wondered, or was this a notion foisted by one upon the others? How, I wondered, did they acquire matchbooks from the Arcadia Motel in Ogden, Utah? Or from the Uranium Club in Grand Junction, Colorado ("the new social center of the uranium community—come in and talk shop"), or Horace's Cafe, in Friarsburg, Tennessee? Or from the Rustic Art Cafe in Dubois, Wyoming? Or from the Istanbul Hilton? Or from Alcatraz? ("World's Finest View of the Golden Gate")?

But I couldn't track them or recapture them as they were. Those fragments left a cold trail—a trail past Savannah's Sapphire Room, past Monticello, past Paradise Point in Gulfport, Mississippi, past the Braden Winch Company in Broken Arrow, Oklahoma, past Chateau Frontenac, past A. W. Kirby's Market at Shively, Kentucky.

I never did get a sense of the family that collected the matchbooks. They're dead and split up now, and I mostly smoked up the matchbooks. What was dear to them never became momentous to me, and I am sorry.

The family that collected those matchbooks could not be tracked and known by its minor artifacts. People are mostly pretty complex. Much about them rests hidden from all others. We are easily lost to each other and sometimes forlorn. We keep on hunting.

I keep on hunting, and not all the time just for myself, not just for myself.

I want to know how it was, want to know what the things I only glimpsed were really like, what the things I never saw or heard might have been. In the moments I can spare, I look in picture books that show old airplanes, hoping to see a plane like that bright red biplane that landed in a field west of Jayton that time so that the pilot—I guess he was a leftover barnstormer—could sell plane rides. Don Jones and I hurried out to see the plane, the first I'd ever seen up close and the only one I'd see up close for years to come. I look for a picture that will show me the bright red biplane, don't find it, but rejoice when I come upon pictures of that beautiful Curtis biplane from the early thirties, the P-6, or maybe views of the Gloster Gladiator, or that wonderful two-engine Grumman fighter, never put into production, the wing and motors forward of the fuselage, the plane disappearing from view except in comic books, where it was flown by the Blackhawks, or maybe even views of the Westland Whirlwind.

I look in picture books that show stills from old movies and wonder what really happened in "Smilin' Through." I saw a preview of that movie once at the TEXAS or KENT or PALACE or TEXAN or whatever theater and was touched by a terrible sadness—was the bride really shot and killed on her wedding day, and how could the groom live with that?—but never saw the movie. And how did it all turn out in "The Mark of Zorro"? I saw maybe two or three episodes of that serial, but not the ending. I don't yet know whether that was because we didn't have the money, or because the theater closed, or because.

And how was it in baseball? I look in picture books and record books wanting to know. How was it with Charley Gehringer and Luke Appling and Arky Vaughan and Paul Waner and Lefty Grove and especially Joe DiMaggio. I heard their names, or read them, but never knew how it was. I still haven't learned, perhaps never will, why sometimes when I heard a quick passage of music on the radio, never knowing what it was or anything except that it was more beautiful than I could believe, I grieved because I thought I'd never hear it again. What I glimpsed or heard for a moment then was lost, I thought. I would never see or hear the like again, I thought, and gone forever.

Why did it strike me so, I wonder? Perhaps I'll never know, not really know. Why was I moved so inexplicably, for God's sake, by the Lux Radio Theater's version of *Wuthering Heights*, wondering if I would never hear such words again? What words did I hear? On the radio, I think Heathcliff said to Cathy, "Don't leave me alone in the dark."

Later, I finally found Emily Brontë's version: "Be with me always—take any form—drive me mad! Only *do* not leave me in this abyss, where I cannot find you!"

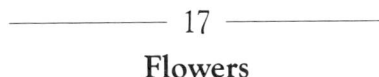

17

Flowers

I look back to catch then or now or hereafter, trying to make a spell that will hold the world. "As if there could be one that worked," Gregory Orr writes in "Near Dawn,"

> I conjure a spell to help
> myself and you who,
> last night in another city,
> fell and cut your scalp—
> eight stitches and you're fine;
> "eggshell thin, a child's skull,"
> the doctor said.
>
> All this
> over the phone from your mother.
>
> Come home, come home; I call
> my wandering ones
> back to my arms—out of dark,
> out of storm, out of endless harm.

My daughter planted the bulbs—I hope I hold her well in mind, hope my memory's true—that spring. That spring before she left. Around the elm. They've come in every year. They're yellow now, the flowers, bright against the green of grass and shrub, against the dark red brick of house. They caught the sun one time and held it close, made light against the dark. She planted the bulbs that spring before she left. They've come in every year. Around the elm. They're yellow now. I saw them when I passed, saw them when I passed.

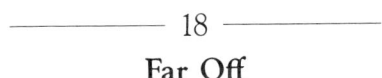

18

Far Off

Sometimes when I hear a child's call, say far down the block past the arching green trees, or maybe way over on the next street and down,

53

or maybe just at twilight, I want to go and be her guard, or his, and teach the child safely home. Sometimes a child calls, far off, maybe just at twilight. Sometimes, I know who the child is and where home is, and want to hold her safe, or him.

19

Places of Which There Is No Knowledge: How History Is Written

When you go back in time, eventually you come up against the place of which there is no knowledge, whether it's prior to some birth, in mistaken memory, in inadequate records, or elsewhere. Eventually, you come to abut that place everywhere. There is no knowledge—there is memory and interpretation, and they are mistaken. You come to abut that place if you go *back*, back before birth, back to Jayton, back to wherever; if you go *out*, say toward others; if you go *sideways*, toward your self as perceived by others, toward your self in other manifestations; if you go *down*, into the subconscious, into the hidden repressed, into the dark known but deliberately hidden; if you go *up* to wherever. We keep learning this, it seems, wherever we look. In his review of Yitzhak Arad's *Belzec, Sobibar, Treblinka*, Michael Marrus asks: "Is this book definitive? For its use of archival sources and its combining of survivors' accounts, one could scarcely ask for more. But we are a long way from understanding the sources of the Nazis' monstrous ambitions or the mechanisms that bound the perpetrators of these crimes together. Mr. Arad's book, with its abundance of horrifying detail, reminds us of how far we have to go."

But I don't know how far I have to go. Is there anything that I already know well, intimately? Can I make a list?

I can make a list of what I presume to know. Others seem sure, seem to know things, seem able to trust their memory. I can make a list of what I presume to know—my pipes, my typewriter, her body, tobacco, okra, weeds, blackeyed peas—but I would be mistaken. About the things I know best, there are things I know not at all. Despite all, I have imagined that they are what I perceive. I have not waited upon them well enough, have not privileged them, have not even privileged myself, for I've been, apparently, oblivious, oblivious as a child and boy, oblivious as a husband and father, oblivious as a scholar and

teacher, unaware then, unaware now of those others and of myself.

What was it for, reading the *Jayton Chronicle?* Jayton was a little town of no note. I didn't know it then and can't know it now, can't find the ones I'm looking for. And what about those I *didn't* look for? What about the missing years? What would I have learned if I had read the missing papers? Nostalgia is an ache for home: we yearn and search for what is not. The *Chronicle* for February 21, 1946, tells me that the American Legion post was named for H. J. Whatley, dead in a prison camp, and Curtis Hancock, killed in a combat air mission. Why wasn't it also named for Jeff Brown and Gatlin Cox? I find Jeff Brown in the Jayton cemetery:

> Brown
>
> In Loving Memory of
> T/Sgt Jeff Brown
> Who Gave Up His Life in
> Devotion to his Country
> 1908–1944
> Greater love hath no man than
> this, that a man lay down his
> life for his friends   JOHN 15–13

But I haven't found Gatlin Cox.

History, Shirley Kaufman says,

> . . . is what we choose
> to remember, peeling the present
> from its skin like a ripe orange,
> juice on our fingers.

Or the mist slipping over
my father where he lies
in one half of his body
unable to speak.

Trying to find the way
is like reading a street sign
in the distance, the letters
blurred and unfocused
until I came closer.

And then I discover
it's only a marker at the border
saying STOP.

What should I have known? Why didn't I know more about the town? Apparently I didn't roam much, except in my own territory. That's startling, but not surprising—all my life I've mostly stayed close, and studied maps more than I've scouted territories. Why didn't I know—I waited fifty years for the *Chronicle* to tell me—that there were regular Trade Days on the square? Why didn't I know and remember more about Jimmy Matthews and Don Jones and Bobby Sproules, more about the canyons, more about school, my classmates, more about the football team that was so glorious in the fall of 1938. Gatlin Cox was on that team, but now I can't find him. They fade, they disappear, they stay in my head. Rodney Jones catches them for a moment in his poem, "Sweep":

The two Garnett brothers who run the Shell station here,
who are working separately just now,
one hunched under the rear axle of Skippy Smith's Peterbilt tractor,
the other humming as he loosens the clamps
to replace my ruptured heater hoses,
have aged twenty years since I saw them last
and want only to talk of high school
and who has died from each class.
Seamless grey sky, horns from the four-lane,
the lot's oil slicks rainbowing and dimpling with rain.
I have been home for three days, listening to an obituary.
The names of relatives met once,
of men from the plant where he works,
click like distant locks on my father's lips.
I know that it's death that obsesses him
more than footfall or weather
and that cancer is far too prevalent
in this green valley of herbicides and chemical factories.
Now Mike, the younger brother,
lifts from my engine compartment

a cluster of ruined hoses,
twisted and curled together like a nest of blacksnakes,
and whistles as he forages in the rack
for more. Slowly, the way things work down here,
while I wait and the rain plinks on the rims of overturned tires,
he and my father trade the names of the dead:
Bill Farrell for Albert Dotson,
Myles Hammond, the quick tackle of our football team,
for Don Appleton, the slow, redheaded one.
By the time the rack is exhausted
I'm thinking if I lived here all year I'd buy American,
I'd drive a truck, and I'm thinking
of football and my father's and Mike's words
staking out an absence I know I won't reclaim.
Because I don't get home much anymore,
I notice the smallest scintilla of change,
every burnt-out trailer and newly paved road,
and the larger, slower change
that is exponential,
that strangeness, like the unanticipated face,
of my aunt, shrunken and perversely stylish
under the turban she wore after chemotherapy.
But mostly it's the wait, one wait after another,
and I'm dropping back deep in the secondary
under the chill and pipe smoke of a cancelled October
while the sweep rolls toward me from the line of scrimmage,
and Myles Hammond, who will think too slowly
and turn his air-force jet into the Arizona desert,
and Don Appleton, who will drive out on a country road
for a shotgun in his mouth, are cut down,
and I'm shifting on the balls of my feet,
bobbing, and saving one nearless hopeless feint,
one last plunge for the blockers
and the ballcarrier who follows the sweep,
and it comes, and comes on.

We wait upon memory to come and tell us the truth, and memory is
always wrong.

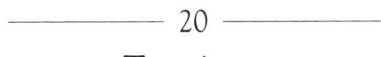

20

Transients

Once, in the spring of 1937, I stayed home from school sick, and a hard,
dark dust storm blew in, though the sun was still there above. That after-

noon, when my brother got off the bus and started home, the dust was blowing so hard that he lost his way and had to backtrack to find home. Later, he swore to me that the sun was shining above the dust and the dust was thick, and he saw his shadow in the air beside him, and I believed him, and I still do. But even if I have it all wrong, brother, we were not shadows in the air, not shadows, brother, not shadows.

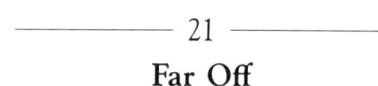

21

Far Off

Sometimes, when I hear a child's call, say far down the block past the arching green trees, or maybe way over on the next street down, or maybe just at twilight, I want to go and be her guard, or his, and teach the child safely home. Sometimes a child calls, far off, maybe just at twilight. Sometimes, I know who the child is and where home is, and want to hold her safe, or him.

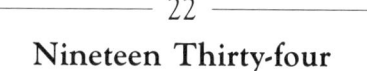

22

Nineteen Thirty-four

Under the headline "Durham-McKinzie," the very first issue in my *Chronicle* collection (that for January 5, 1934) reports that on December 22, 1933, Miss Willie Mae Durham and Mr. J. E. McKinzie were married. The bride, who wore a "charming ensemble of blue and white," was, so the report continues, "the charming and talented daughter of Mr. and Mrs. Ernest Durham of the Duck Creek community." This news mattered to me.

Miss Willie Mae Durham is my Aunt Bill. I don't know who decided to call her Willie Mae, and I don't know who later decided to call her Bill, but that's who she is, and Mr. and Mrs. Ernest Durham were my Grandpa and Grandma.

And more: the news helped me a little to locate myself in time. If Grandma and Grandpa were already in the Duck Creek community —it's north of Jayton—in December, 1933, then my earliest fragmented recollections of them in that other farmhouse east of Jayton go back much earlier than I had thought. But no matter for now.

And in the issue for Friday, April 27, 1934, sweet Peggy Sue shows up. Apparently she didn't always live in Jayton. Apparently she came to Jayton somewhere around the time my family moved there. Among the "Personals" in that issue is this: "Baker Robinson's children, Bake Jr., Dickey [he's the one who would be called 'Red' later and who would be my brother's best friend], and Peggy Sue, of Stamford spent last week end here with relatives." Does that mean that the children lived apart from the father? If it does, I didn't know, Peggy Sue.

Page four of the issue for October 5, 1934, is given over entirely to this:

WATCH FOR
STARTLING ANNOUNCEMENT
TO APPEAR
IN THE
NEXT ISSUE OF
"THE CHRONICLE"

I guess I will never know the news — the next issue, for October 12, is missing.

THE NEWS

I judge that Mr. Wade, the owner and editor, felt free to editorialize wherever he wanted to in the paper. The issue for January 19, 1934, told of "the big idea behind the 1934–1935 government cotton plan" — to cut down the eleven-million-bale carryover from the previous growing season by reducing cotton acreage by 40 percent. The cotton farmer was to be protected "from decreasing income while he does this by paying him the money collected from a 4-cent per pound processing tax on all domestically used cotton." On the front page of the next issue (January 26), under the headline "Determined to hang," this appears:

> Is there a single sane reason why the Government should pay any man for doing the one thing that common sense tells him he should do?
> The idea of paying a farmer to reduce his cotton acreage is all wrong. If he won't do the thing that good judgment tells him to do, then he should be penalized for not doing it instead of being paid to do it.

Mr. Wade notwithstanding, the issue for February 2 reports that up to January 16, some 15,465 bales had been ginned (against a yearly average reported by the *Texas Almanac* of 12,500 bales). And Mr. Wade notwithstanding, plans for reduction continued; on March 23, the paper announced that 5,395,291 acres in Texas were to be retired from cotton production, and on May 25, a front-page story spelled out the chief features of the Bankhead Act restricting American cotton production. A brief note on October 26 predicts "the smallest yield of this territory since 1918."

The year 1934 wasn't a particularly good year in West Texas. It wasn't anything special much of anywhere. The *Chronicle* that year carried frequent notices of sheriff's sales of property. On June 29 this notice appeared: "DON'T FORGET: –The Yellow Cat and the Mattress Factory Properties will be sold by the state at Clairemont July 3rd, Tuesday, to the highest bidder. R. I. Goodall, Sheriff, Kent County." The July 6 issue reported that the Yellow Cat, an old hotel, brought $205, and the mattress factory went for $46. Money, or the lack of it, was often in the news.

Mr. Wade was apparently not always fully in favor of various forms of government relief. On February 2, this appeared:

> There are very few, if any, rural sections of the United States in better condition than Kent County, Texas. However, here, as elsewhere, there is some need for relief work and some justification for small-scale relief projects. But, if one were to judge by the list of applicants for both direct and work relief, he would believe that the county was populated in a large measure by a destitute and poverty stricken people.
>
> The truth of the matter is that what was intended as a godsend to the needy lies in great danger of becoming prostituted to serve the interests of those both undeserving and unworthy.

The issue for March 9 announced regulations for making emergency crop loans (a farmer could get up to $250 "if he cannot qualify for credit elsewhere"); on March 30 notice of federal land bank loans appeared; the issue for May 4 told of an extension until May 15 for crop loan applications; and the June 22 issue announced that winter wheat loans were now available. A notice from the county relief roll administrator in the September 14 paper says that the county is still in a position to help those who are unable to work, "but those who are able to work, we only have for you a cotton sack, so please do not come to us expecting any other help." A story in the next column says, "We are informed that farmers are now paying 75 cents per hundred for cotton picking and as a result most everyone that is able is to be found in the cotton fields this week."

At 75 cents per hundred, no one was going to get noticeably rich. The statement of the First State Bank published in the July 13 issue shows resources of $64,195.91, of which $3,990.73 is "cash in the bank."

Drought relief stories occur frequently, and then more frequently. The issue for July 13 says that drought relief work will start soon; on July 20 we get the regulations governing drought relief loans, the issue for July 26 reprints an item from the *Texas Weekly* asking for mutual understanding so that both those on relief and those administering relief funds can maintain some self-respect and dignity. The same issue announces that students can now pay their tuition on the installment plan at John Tarleton Agricultural College (now Tarleton State University) by making four payments (from nine to twenty-eight dollars) through the term. On October 19, the state relief director warns county administrators to observe the new law requiring that at least thirty-five percent of the state funds allotted to the county must be spent on "the construction, repair or maintenance of lateral roads or other work projects."

The *Chronicle* for November 16 carries notice that "heads of Texas families on relief rolls who can not resist the temptation of alcoholic liquors or the lure of gambling games will not receive cash grants under a policy announced today by the Texas Relief Commission," but the same issue notifies county administrators that Maine Irish potatoes (in surplus) are available for distribution to the needy, and a later issue (November 28) announces that rice is also available for distribution.

The News — Local and Personal

Aunt Bill's husband shows up in the September 14 paper with a warning notice: "All parties with wolf hounds are hereby notified to keep out of the McKenzie pastures north and east of Jayton as all that territory is in a State Game Preserve, stocked with deer by the State.— A word to the wise is sufficient." It is signed by J. E. McKenzie, Jr., the name now spelled with an *e* instead of an *i* as it was in January. The same September issue tells about Mr. J. W. Clark, now celebrating with his wife their fiftieth wedding anniversary. Back in 1901, it seems, Mr. Clark was a cook on the Matador Ranch. He was pressed into service when the Baptists held a conference up in Dickens County (next north of Kent County). By his recollection he cooked eighteen hundred biscuits.

This issue also provides two columns of jokes. Sample: "'What is that new building you've put up on the hill there?' asked a curious city visitor of a farmer. 'Well,' replied the farmer, 'if I can find a tenant for it, it's a bungalow, if I can't, it's a barn.'" Second sample: "*Conductor*—'Can't you see that No Smoking sign?' *Passenger*—'Sure, but there's another says Wear Our Corsets so I ain't paying no attention to any of 'em.'"

The January 19 issue carries this headline: "Clyde Barrow Frees His Pals In Daring Prison Break." On May 25, we learn that Clyde and Bonnie Parker have been killed, and the next paper (June 1) reprints a letter from Mrs. Hollabaugh's daughter in Dallas. She's been to the undertaking establishment to see the bodies and reports that "the undertaker had to embalm the pieces and place them together," and that "while they did a wonderful job, one could tell that the bodies were just pieced together." The October 26 issue reports that "Pretty Boy" Floyd has also been killed.

Mostly, though, I notice things that I should have known about, but didn't, or knew about and forgot.

For example, I wonder why I didn't know about First Mondays. I can't tell whether or not this was a regular event through the years, but there are frequent references to First Monday. The first issue in my file, for January 5, 1934, tells about the second First Monday held in Jayton. Monday would have been January 1. The events sound like something a boy would eventually hear about and attend and maybe even join in. I wonder why I never heard of First Monday.

On that First Monday in 1934, there was a prize given for the best matched team and for the largest ham, and there were first, second, and third prizes for cakes. Then, "Five Guineas were turned free at the judges' stand and each person catching one and returning it to the judges' stand received $1.00. We were unable to secure the names of the winners in this event, but Prof. Coons made a spectacular catch that is deserving of mention." When I knew him from afar, Prof. Coons was the superintendent of the Jayton schools. Later, there was a rodeo. I can understand not knowing about this particular First Monday—I would have been four years old, and maybe my family was not yet even in Jayton—but I don't know why I didn't know about others in the following years. I wonder why I wasn't there, or maybe went and then forgot.

I don't remember the New Deal Cafe, either. It reopened Saturday, March 10, after being redecorated by the new owners. I don't remember, or never knew, that by action of the town council (reported on April 13), "all male inhabitants of the Town of Jayton, between the ages of twenty-one and forty-five years, shall be liable to work on the streets and public alleys of the town of Jayton. . . ." Some exemptions were possible; otherwise, all the eligible men could be called for five days a year. I wonder if later my father went and worked on the streets and public alleys while I never knew or noticed.

But I couldn't have known about the archeological team that came down on Sunday, May 13, from Texas Tech in Lubbock to investigate a site on the Brazos between Jayton and Clairemont where local citizens had found "an Indian pot of unusual design." On the way to the site, the team stopped at the Harrison farm to see what they determined to be the jawbone of a mammoth, then went on to what turned out to be an Indian camping ground. The county existed before I did, and otherwise.

The issue for July 7 gives notice of new highway construction (later, when it was all finished, the road would split the town square and go on to Spur) and lists available jobs and salaries. The highest rate went to shovel operators, at $6.00 a day, the lowest to common laborers at $2.60, a cook and a watchman at $2.40, and a waterboy at $2.00. By the time my father worked for a while on the road a couple of years later, wages had gone down some.

And why didn't I know until I read the July 20 issue that there was a city pump, now fixed and working? And just in time, too, the *Chronicle* reports, for "Credit Lake was down to a soupy condition and in another week the town would have been completely out of stock water."

On Wednesday, September 26 (reported September 28), the new bridge over the Double Mountain Fork of the Brazos was opened. It wasn't always there, except to me, maybe.

The paper for October 19 reports that a museum team from San Antonio found a Folsom point in digs on the west bank of the Salt Fork of the Brazos, about ten miles south of Jayton, and I learn from the November 2 issues that Mayme Morris Murphy was on the sick list early in the week. Later, she would be my first-grade teacher and get married and then be Mayme Morris Murphy Fowler.

The Yellow Cat shows up again on November 28. Jayton's first hotel, sold in 1934 for taxes, it's now being torn down. It had become, the paper says, a "refuge in time of stress for all the drifting population of Jayton." I still don't know exactly where it was.

Sometimes, when I look, I see a strange world. Sometimes, I don't see it at all: it's long gone.

 I can't catch the meat-canning demonstration reported in the January 5 issue. It included steak, roast, meat loaf, liver paste, and sausage. Or the revenuers' raid over in Stonewall County, reported on February 9, or the related story on February 16: "You had better dismiss your private bootlegger after February 11th if he is pedaling liquor on which no federal tax has been paid, for you will be just as guilty as he is. . . ." Or make the "flying trip" reported on March 23:

> Tuesday evening, L. H. Mason asked us to go to Girard with him. He was driving one of those new '34 knee action Chevrolets and upon assuring us that 30 minutes was all the time it required we gladly accepted the ride, but we told him that if he did not make it as promised we would fine him a cold drink.
> Sufficient to say: we did not get the drink, for we made it in 29½ minutes and spent ten of those in Girard. We call that a flying trip.

And I can't go to the cemetery working, as reported on May 4 and regularly thereafter.

 To me, now, driving through the territory he mentions in the May 18 issue, it looks lonesome, but Mr. Wade called it in the headline "A Land of New Homes and New Hopes":

> Monday of this week, in company with H. D. Black, L. H. Mason, and H. E. Duncan, the editor had the pleasure of visiting what we believe is going to be the banner farming section of Jayton's trade territory. The trip was made by the four mentioned above for the purpose of securing the necessary signers for a petition to the Post Office department to approve a mail route for the

territory Northeast from Jayton to the Ward Ranch in Stonewall county.

In making the rounds we covered 56 miles and without doubt saw as fine a section of farming country as is to be found in Texas. Just the exact number of acres now under cultivation it is impossible to give, but we are of the opinion that no part of the trade territory of the town can or ever will surpass the acreage in the territory we covered in our trip of Monday.

Golden Pond, Salt Flat, the Ward Ranch and the Pursley Ranch communities are all included in the proposed new mail route. . . .

When they got to the Gus Smith place, Mr. Wade reports, though Mrs. Smith was sick, "nothing would do Gus but that we stop for noon lunch." The group accepted the invitation,

and fell out for noon. Mason proved to be a good hand with a skillet, and also with a coffee pot; Lonnie Smith, who was visiting with Gus, turned in and made two pans of fine biscuits; Black set the table; and when all was ready the editor and Duncan did most of the eating—Black being able to put away only six slices of ham, three cups of coffee, a gallon of milk, and a half-pan of bread. Mason did his best, but quit one cup of coffee behind Black. Duncan and the editor took care of the rest.

Salt Flat shows up in the next week's issue, too: "If you want to get in on the ground floor, see Cafe Brown who is promoting a new town site at Salt Flat." It didn't work.

Meanwhile, down at the Methodist church, according to the June 15 paper, they were holding services on a schedule unlike any I remember —Sunday school at ten, okay, and a special Father's Day service at eleven, okay, with the center section reserved for fathers, but then there was also a service at three and another at eight-thirty. What were the Methodists up to? I learn later, in the September 28 paper, that the Stonewall Baptist Association was going to meet on October 8 at the Salt Flat Church. I wonder where it was and what became of it. In town, I guess the Baptists were temporarily without a preacher. The October 19 issue gives the program for Sunday services, and it's all done by lay people— my Aunt Bill is down for the devotional, and Don Jones's mother is listed for a talk.

It sometimes seems a strange world, a far world, maybe best a gone world. The June 22 paper reports that "'Juneteenth' passed off very quietly in Jayton, with the negroes celebrating very little if any."

But on Sunday, July 22, there was a Kent County Singing Convention up at Girard, and on September 23 the Tri-County Singing Convention held its annual meeting at Jayton.

Some stranger, maybe, passing through, maybe, never made it. The June 8 paper carries this story:

> A dead man was found last Sunday afternoon in a pasture on the OS Ranch, directly west of Polar, near the county line. Investigations made by the county officials went to show that he had been dead for possibly six months and about all that was left of the man was his skeleton.
>
> The remains were inclined against a tree in a position that led the officer to believe that he had lain down and gone to sleep possibly dying while asleep. There was no evidence of violence. The head was separate from the body, having been dragged, supposedly by some varmint, about 15 feet away. He was wearing a pair of overalls, a jumper, underclothes, a heavy mackinaw, but no shirt. He also wore a pair of heavy shoes. There was found on him a pipe, two radiator caps, and some other odds and ends.
>
> A letter was found, but it carried no address, but was signed "your little old sis, Ola Powell." The letter spoke of sending a box of fruit for Christmas and enclosed a self-addressed, stamped envelope, but the envelope was gone.
>
> He was a large man, more than middle aged, apparently dark complexioned, the teeth in the upper right jaw were missing.
>
> The body was found by Roy Wright who was hunting for a lost cow.
>
> Interment was made in the Polar Cemetery.

He must have been awfully tired. I guess he got as far as he could go. He lay down in a desolate place, and it became more desolate. I wonder what became of Ola? Did he use that stamped envelope to send her a letter?

INTERLUDE ON THE STATE OF THE ART IN JOURNALISM

Mr. Wade, I judge, wasn't shy, and I guess he wasn't bound by any recommendations about journalistic style except his own. Writing about the upcoming Texas Interscholastic League meet on February 16, he says, "Folks, it won't be long until the track meet is history, so let's make records before the sand blows. March 8–10 are the dates and Girard is the place." An obituary in the March 2 paper begins, "The Death Angel came into our midst on Friday. . . ." On March 9, this: "The Chronicle force desires to apologize to Mrs. W. J. Garrett for the omission last week of an important program she phoned in to us. The chief flunkey was taken ill Wednesday afternoon and the relief man could not translate his scribbling and the article was left on the hook. We regret this omission very much."

The same issue carries a tasteless joke about one Rastus. What we would call ugly racism, vile prejudice, must, I judge, have seemed natural and non-controversial. The front page of the April 6 paper carries this headline: "Dark Meat Carved As Two Dusky Females Fight." The second-level headline says, "Fracas in Mill Flats Almost Fatal to Two Negro Women."

The news otherwise is diverse and, I guess, according to the editor's temper. The front page for May 4 announces that "this week L. O. Mayer has on display at his place of business, the last horse that worked in Texas on a fire wagon. He is a freaky looking old critter and is attracting much comment." On June 1, mixed in with the "Personals," this appears: "What we need in this country right now is a RAIN." In the "Personals" for October 19 this observation occurs: "With eggs at 25 cents per dozen, the love of custard pie has had a decided drop." And on November 28, Mr. Wade remarks in the "Personals" that "When you argue with a fool, he is doing the same thing."

And Now, the Weather

On January 19, the *Chronicle* reports that the weather this winter has been abnormally warm and dry, and probably accounts for the "considerable sickness abroad in the land." On February 23 a report from Plainview tells of a sandstorm so fierce up there in the Panhandle that a man whose car stalled with a busted carburetor twelve miles outside of town was able to "sail" his car in on the wind. The March 2 issue, however, tells of a "gentle rain of 12 hours duration" that has left everyone rejoicing.

It didn't last, not in 1934. Just a little later, on March 23, a front-page report headlined "Water! Water! Water" says, "The greatest need of this entire county is water. Good clean wholesome pure drinking water, and water for all homes, town, farm and ranch homes alike." On April 20, we learn that it has rained *three* times within the last thirty days, the most recent a "trash-moving, clod-dissolving, soaking rain." Still, by June 1, Mr. Wade is asking for RAIN, and in the June 15 issue, he is reporting on the "Worst Drought in History of Country." The same issue reports on a sandstorm that came in on Tuesday, June 12:

Sandy Tuesday Night Cools Atmosphere

After three days of terrible heat that sapped the strength of man, beast and growing crops, a sandy came from the West Tuesday night carrying tons of dirt, a great deal of electricity and a few scattering rain drops that cooled the atmosphere considerably.

If the dust and sand had been rain, we would have had plenty of moisture Wednesday morning, and as it is, we are just a little cooler and a lot dirtier with no bath water!

A front-page story the next week (June 22) carries the headline, "Will It Rain In Time?" A note on June 29 offers this: "Farmers in Kent County need not worry about having to pay the tax of five cents a pound for all cotton produced over the county's allotment. Ten more days of dry weather and one more sandstorm and there will not be enough cotton left in the county to produce enough lint to make a pair of overalls." On July 20, Mr. Wade reports that "the organized churches of Texas are calling on all their members to pray for rain" in the midst of "the worst drouth from one end of the state to the other that it has ever known." The item ends with this:

> The rivers, the creeks, the wells, the cisterns and the tanks are dry. The crops that were so promising in the early months of the year are now fast turning to naked stems and the fields are becoming barren wastes of sand and parched earth. It can now truly be said, "God, give us rain, or we die."

As late as October 26, Mr. Wade reports that the town council has arranged through the Public Works Administration to have the city lake cleaned "so that if it ever rains enough to put water in it, the water will be fit to use for domestic purposes."

Entertainment

As the year began, "Gold Diggers of 1933" was playing down at the Palace Theater—the same theater that I thought had always and forever been called the Texas. In February, "big time vaudeville" came to the theater up at Spur—Buck Cathey's Spot light Revue. On March 9, Mr. Wade picked up a story from Dallas reckoning, according to one insurance actuarial department, that Mae West, by reminding women that it was all right to have curves, had probably helped to improve their health. Mr. Wade observed that all men had already approved of Miss West's curves.

On March 30, the *Chronicle* reports that the Allerita–Loomis tent theater players would be in town for three days the following week, their feature play to be *The Girl from the Nudist Colony*. On May 11, the manager of the Palace announces that he has to cut back for the summer and will run only one picture a week for the Saturday matinee, Saturday night, and Sunday afternoon showings. He hoped to resume full-time showings in the fall: we all hope things get better come picking time. On May 25, a notice says that the young people from the Methodist church are going to put on a stunt night at the Palace on May 31.

I suppose that picking time didn't bring good news to the Palace owner. The issue for October 5 tells that the theater is to open under new management, and the issue for October 19 carries an advertisement, with no name given for the theater, for the week's shows — Friday and Saturday, Tim McCoy in "Beyond the Law," Sunday and Monday, "Call It Luck," and Thursday only, Marlene Dietrich in "The Scarlet Empress." The October 26 paper carries this: "Miss Eulalah Goodman, of this place, is the lucky winner of three months free admission to the Avalon Theater here as a result of the contest sponsored by the new management to rename the theater." First it was the PALACE, which it never was in my mind. Now it's the AVALON, which it can't be in my mind. I guess it will never be the TEXAS, which it always was in my mind.

SPORTS

The track meet was held in Girard, just as Mr. Wade announced, and the issue for March 16 reports that Jayton won the high school meet, that is to say, the all-round championship, including the scholastic contests.

On May 11, a notice appeared asking baseball fans to meet on Monday, May 14, down at the Palace, to organize a baseball club. And on May 18, Mr. Wade says, "Let's go, folks, because Jayton's gonna PLAY BALL!" I am not entirely certain that it's *baseball*; as I grew part of the way up, the words *baseball* and *softball* were both used when one talked about softball. I think it's baseball. The June 1 issue carried word of a victory over Rotan, 7–3; the June 8 issue reports a 13–11 triumph over Peacock, and the next issue (June 15) tells of a second win over Peacock. The June 22 paper reports that fans and business houses are supporting the team, though they have now just lost to Peacock by 11 to 2. From the July 13 paper I learn that the team has now beat Peacock again, and also Aspermont, but the next week's paper reports a loss.

I don't know whether or not that's the end of this season. It is the end of what my file of *Chronicles* will tell me. I do know that Mc-Adoo came to town on Sunday, July 29, to engage Jayton in a donkey ball game, but I have not been able to learn the score.

THE MARKET REPORT

The *Chronicle* for February 16 shows that over at Mayer Auto Service, you could get tires from $5.50 to $9.40. Down at the Red and White Grocery, a no. 2 can of hominy cost 12 cents, and a dozen bananas cost 25 cents. Dr. E. L. Alexander has his office at Huls Drug Store, office phone 30, so a small notice proclaims. Jay-Mason Chevrolet announced that their chief mechanic had been attending a special school for Chevrolet mechanics at Abilene. Bryant-Link Company offered "Charming new Spring Coats and the ever popular Swagger Suits" at $13.95 up, "Men's fade-proof Dress shirts, extra nice, only $1.45, and a few nice topcoats, extra special," at $14.95. Robinson Brothers Undertakers offered caskets, coffins, funeral supplies/hearse furnished when desired/will meet all out-of-town prices. Elsewhere, in a bigger display advertisement, Robinson's ("Everything From the Cradle to the Grave") says this at the top:

WHO IS AFRAID OF THE BIG BAD WOLF?
There was a time when most of us were "afraid of the big bad wolf," but that time is past. Confidence has been restored and courage has driven out all fear.
Steadily we go forward and every step gives us additional assurance that better days are here again.
The pick-up in our business proves this to us every day. It is positively gratifying when our old customers come in and purchase their needs with confidence.
It's showing on their faces – confidence born of ready cash they have in their pockets.

In the next column, West Texas Utilities is offering laundry equipment.

I see by the paper for July 6 that Robinson's has salad dressing at 25 cents for a quart jar, a pound of coffee at 22 cents, and a forty-eight-pound sack of flour for $1.70. Jones Drug Store has this notice:

CHICKENS – TURKEY
Don't wait and have diseased fowls from Worms and Losses from Blood Sucking Lice, Mites, Fleas and Blue Bugs this Spring. Begin NOW to give STAR PARASITE REMOVER in their drinking water for both fowls and baby chicks. It will keep them free of these destructive

Parasites, their system toned up, their health and egg production
good at a very small cost—or money refunded.

In the same issue, Jay-Mason Chevrolet has new cars for $465.00 and
up, and Bryant-Link Company has silk dresses for $3.95, silk hose for
89 cents, one group of $1.49 wash dresses, special for only $1.00, men's
dress shirts for 89 cents, (well down from February), men's overalls for
98 cents, men's summer suits for $8.95, sheets for $1.00, and bath towels
for 19 cents.

On September 28, Landers' Grocery advertised three bars of toilet
soap for 10 cents, a half-gallon of syrup for 29 cents, and 10 pounds
of spuds for 25 cents. Across the square, Robinsons was advertising 100
pounds of no. 1 grade spuds for $1.85 (a bargain if you could lift the
sack), a gallon of new crop sorghum for 60 cents, a pound carton of lard
for 70 cents, and a half-gallon bucket of jelly, any flavor, for 35 cents.

By November 28, Robinson's has a dozen bananas at 17 cents (down
from 25 cents in February), 100 pounds of sugar for 95 cents, a quart
of mustard for 15 cents, and a pound of cocoa for 12 cents. Higher on
the page Mrs. Ivey F. Murdoch, phone 37, says she is "never too rushed
to do your beauty work as it should be done." Jones Drug Store opens
its advertisement with this:

WE ARE THANKFUL
Yes we are truly thankful for the friendship, confidence and
patronage of the many who have known us since our childhood.
It shall be our purpose to continue to merit this confidence as long
as we are permitted to serve you as your druggist.
For you we wish only the best—long life—Health—Happiness
and Prosperity.

Nose drops, with atomizer, are available for 69 cents, a large tube of
toothpaste and a "transparent barrel GOLD BANDED FOUNTAIN PEN" come
at 59 cents, and a bottle of 100 aspirins costs 39 cents.

Sometimes, when I look, I see a strange world. Sometimes, I don't
see it at all: it's long gone.

23

Missing Issues

I have no copies of the *Chronicle* for 1935. I wonder how things were,
and what the news was, and what I might have learned from the missing issues.

In 1936 I started to school, I guess, but otherwise have no news. No copies of the *Chronicle* survived as late as Mr. Parker's microfilm. I wonder how things were, and what the news was, and what I might have learned from the missing issues.

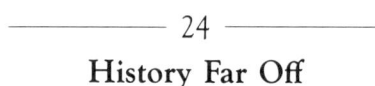

24

History Far Off

> The historian is both discoverer and creator. To the uniqueness of his role we have a clue in the very word "history," which means both the course of the past and the legible account of the past. The historian is always trying to reduce, or remove, that ambiguity. If he is successful, he leads his readers to take – or mistake – his account for what was really there.
>
> DANIEL J. BOORSTIN

Were we shadows in the air, brother, shadows, with no one left to testify that we were there?

> The historian sets himself a dangerous, even an impossible, task. In the phrase of the great Dutch historian J. H. Huizinga, he is "a wrestler with the angel." It is the angel of death who makes his work necessary yet destined never to be definitive. If man were not mortal, we would not be deprived of the living testimony of the actors, and so required to give new form to the receding infinity.
>
> DANIEL J. BOORSTIN

And who will hear the child call from far off?

> Historians can rediscover the past only by the relics it has left from the present. They try to convince us that the relics they have examined and interpreted in their narrative are reliable samples of the experience people really had. But how reliable are the remains of the past as clues to what was really there?
>
> My life as a historian has brought me vivid reminders of how partial is the remaining evidence of the whole human past, how casual and how accidental is the survival of its relics.
>
> DANIEL J. BOORSTIN

What would I have learned, I wonder, if I had read the missing papers?

---------------- 25 ----------------

Nineteen Thirty-seven

Under the heading "Jayton's Personal Items" in the *Chronicle* for August 5, 1937, I found my other Grandpa: "Mr. R. B. Corder has sold the Jayton Mattress factory to Mr. Suggs who is adding new machinery and getting ready for a big fall and winter run of mattress making." I think I knew that he ran the mattress factory for a while, but I had altogether forgotten until I saw the notice.

Then in the issue for September 9, I came upon this notice: "Mr. and Mrs. J. E. McKinzie are the proud parents of a new girl born Thursday night at Lubbock Sanitarium." That's my Aunt Bill again and Uncle J. E., his name once again back to the *i*. The new girl mentioned is my cousin Carol Ann. She's pretty. I don't think I ever knew the date of her birth, but the announcement appeared in the paper for Thursday, September 9, and it says she was born Thursday night, so I reckon it was Thursday, September 2. Anyway, she's pretty. Maybe one of the missing papers told about her older brother, William Harvey. I didn't find him.

THE NEWS

On February 4, the *Chronicle* reports that on January 30, "Jayton was well represented at the President's Ball at Spur last Saturday night and a great time was reported by those who attended." Thirty-two people from Jayton went up to see FDR into his second term.

Though the news otherwise doesn't indicate that many people were prospering noticeably, I see in the issue for June 24 that deposits in the Jayton bank are up substantially: "We notice in the news carried in the *Abilene Reporter* that bank deposits at Rotan had increased $170,000 since the bringing in of the big oil well at that place. This caused us to wonder just how Jayton's bank was stacking up in comparison even though we have no oil wells. Well it may surprise some folks, nevertheless it is true, the deposits in the Jayton bank have increased $60,000 within the last twelve months to a day." (More news later about oil wells.)

An item on July 15 reports a new flying record: "Setting a new non-stop distance record, the Russian trans-polar fliers landed their big monoplane near San Jacinto, California, about 6:30 a.m. Wednesday

[July 7] after covering almost 6,700 miles in their daring flight from Moscow, over the top of the world to the United States. The long flight was made in a little more than 63 hours."

Some things seemed to be going along all right. Some didn't. The *Chronicle* announces on December 9 that "cash benefits to the qualified unemployed will become payable on January 1, from a reserve fund built up by Texas employers since the establishment of the Texas Unemployment Commission a year ago."

Earlier, the stretch of the new Highway 18 to Jayton (just barely) had been completed. The highway remained on Mr. Wade's mind—and, I guess, indirectly, on mine, for in the spring of 1937 my family had moved to the little house not far from Spur and near Grandpa Durham's farm, so that my father could work on the highway. The issue for October 7, later that year after we had already moved back to Jayton when the oil mill opened again, reports that the stretch of the highway from Spur to the Kent County line was now complete and open. A little later (on October 21) the *Chronicle* is hopeful: "Highway 18 will soon be open to the traveling public from Spur to Peacock. It is open now from Spur to the Kent County line and from Jayton to Peacock and could be opened from Jayton to Girard but there is a little more work to be done on the road from Girard to the Dickens County line. Ten more days should see this work completed." The November 4 issue says that the road is open, but not all of it is hard-surfaced yet.

And sure enough, oil was a topic of some interest. The paper for July 15 reports that Gulf Oil Corporation is trying to lease up to 20,000 acres, at a dollar per acre, for oil exploration in northwestern Kent County. On July 29, an item indicates that leasing goes on. Explorations in the Rotan field, a big center of interest, encouraged folks' attention, I judge. Then on September 30, the *Chronicle* reports a 13,000-barrel gusher—the eighth well in the new field—near Rotan. By November 4, the paper is hopeful again: "Developments of an encouraging nature have taken place within the past ten days which lead us to believe that from one to three wells will be under contract for drilling within the next thirty days in acreage blocked around Jayton that comes right up to the city limits on two sides."

Interesting as oil was, cotton was a more frequent and compelling topic for the *Chronicle*.

On February 4, Mr. Wade could still say that things looked pretty good—farm cash income was up 64 percent since 1933; forced farm sales had been cut in half; farm real estate values were up 12 percent. On

July 12, he is interpreting the County Agricultural Conservation Committee's rules on acreage devoted to cotton as a soil-depleting crop. By August 5, the *Chronicle* reports the earliest bale of cotton in the county's history, in on July 28, and further reports that Jayton gins were ready for a bumper crop: "The heavy throbbing of large diesel engines merging with the rhythmic hum of gin machinery as the power was turned on in the cotton gins here this week broadcast the news to farmers in the territory that Jayton's three gins are tuned up and ready to handle the new cotton crop. Smoke poured from the stack of the Jayton Cooperative Gin as visual evidence of that plant's readiness."

All three of the gin managers were optimistic. One remarked that "after a good night, the cotton looks like it had had a rain. I have never seen a crop stand up as well in such dry, hot weather." On August 26, an item reminded farmers to keep their cotton gin tickets on the likelihood that subsidy payments would be made for the crop grown in 1937, and on September 2, the paper announced that the government would make loans of nine cents a pound on the year's cotton crop. Instructions for loan applications were clarified in the September 23 issue. By September 30, the gins had handled over a thousand bales. By October 14, some two thousand bales had been yarded. On October 21, a headline said, "Ginners Give Warning Against Green Cotton," with this notice following:

> Ginners all over this section are issuing warnings to cotton growers to not be in too great haste to harvest their fleecy staple from maturing fields.
>
> It is said to be mechanically impossible for any gin to turn out good results from wet or green cotton. It cannot be properly cleaned, when wet or green the gin has a tendency to cut the staple and make a "ropy" sample, and there is also considerable shrinkage in both the cotton and the cottonseed, all meaning a considerable loss to the grower and may be obviated by simply waiting until cotton is dryer before bringing it to the gin.

Apparently the problem was serious: in the same issue a full-page advertisement appeared, sponsored by the three gins in Jayton and two in Girard, warning cotton producers not to bring in wet or green cotton. On November 11, the paper remarks that drizzle and colder temperatures were holding up the cotton harvest. The same story observes that "even the Congress of the United States is getting wise to the fact that to control the cotton crop more than acreage control will have to be considered"—farmers had made more cotton on fewer acres.

What with one thing and another, things looked a little better and looked a little worse.

Suggestions about soil and water conservation occur frequently. The issue for February 25 carries several items: one reports on payments to farmers under the 1937 Agricultural Program (under Class 1, for example, a farmer could receive payments by transferring up to thirty-five percent of his acreage from cotton to a soil-conserving crop); a second item reported on the progress of terracing in the county; a third encouraged farmers to use trench silos for storage. Trench silos show up again: a story in the July 15 issue recommends them as storage for feed crops, and another on July 22 urges farmers to store while the feed is right. The March 11 paper announces that enrollments will be accepted in April for the Civilian Conservation Corps. On October 21, the county agent is trying to teach farmers to store water by terracing, but already, on August 26, it may have been too late: "Too bad that all the cultivated land in Kent County was not terraced and the rows run on contour during our recent rains. Had this been the case many of the farms would have stored up in the soil a vast supply of water which will probably be needed by the crop next July and August. Had the land been well terraced much of the valuable top soil which was being washed from the farm by the run off water would still be on the farm instead of in the creek and river bottoms. The gulleys would not be in the field."

And the *Chronicle* often remarked a regular absence of money. On January 28, this appeared:

A Dirty Deal

Four sevenths of the folks in Kent County were removed from the Old Age Assistance rolls this month. If this same average held good over the entire state, then more than 50,000 of the state's 90,000 that were on the rolls are out in the cold today.

The Austin report said about 11 thousand were cut off in the entire state, which if true, convinces us that Kent County has been given a dirty deal. We do not know who is to blame, we only wish we could find out.—Oh! Man!

The old folks in Kent County are just as deserving as the old folks in any other county in the state. No more. No less. And why they should be given the hot end of the poker is more than ye Ed can understand.

In 1937, relief was more than Rolaids. In the February 4 issue, this appeared:

The Relief Situation

A relief administrator in a certain county, in a certain state, was filling out the customary application for a large and humorless woman of middle age.

"Do you owe any back house rent?" asked the administrator.

"Mister, we may be needing relief," answered the woman with simple dignity, "but I'll have you to know that we've at least got modern plumbing."

The February 25 issue reports that new regional administration is working to restore some of the old folks to the rolls.

The March 11 paper describes proposed help for farmers from the federal Department of Agriculture, urges farmers to keep the prescribed work sheets, and reports that sixty-one percent of Kent County farmers are tenant farmers. The March 18 issue announces that Kent County farmers are to receive $35,419.73 in relief, 208 out of 403 applicants to get checks for complying with conservation programs. By October 21, the paper reports that farm loans can be renewed. On November 4, we learn that old age pensions will not be reduced, and that the local post office will process unemployment reports. Things looked a little better and looked a little worse.

The State of the Art in Journalism

I remember, and the paper affirms, that Mr. Wade was the owner and publisher of the *Jayton Chronicle*. I expect he was also editor, staff writer, columnist, proofreader, and sometimes janitor. It's not too surprising that he would feel free to say what he pleased in the paper. On Thursday, September 30, this appeared on the front page: "Right now, while all the population of Mexico is in Texas picking cotton, would be a good time for the U.S. to annex Mexico." He didn't always, I judge, feel a strong need to start every story with the five Ws. On October 21, a story under the headline, "Thieves Ply Their Trade in Jayton," began with this: "While honest folks sleep in West Texas, thieves ply their trade. Last week they came into Kent County and from four different farms assembled 1000 pounds of seed cotton and high-tailed it to a place unknown."

The News—Local and Personal

The issue for December 16, Thursday, offers announcements of Christmas programs and surprise to me. I can't quite be sure of some events. Did the Methodists' pageant, "The Great Gift," occur on Sunday, December 19, or on Sunday, December 26? I'm pretty sure of the Baptists' pageant, presented Wednesday, December 22, at seven-thirty. I'm pretty sure that's when my brother, by then all of thirteen, sang a solo rendition of "We Three Kings." I still don't know how he did it. What surprises me is that on Friday, December 24, at five-thirty, down in the town square, there was a public Christmas program. Santa Claus was there in person. I have no recollection at all of the occasion. Did my family not go? Why, if that's the case, wasn't I out wandering around, and why didn't I stop by? Did I go and lose the whole occasion from my mind?

There's every reason I should have known about the Christmas events, but few or no reasons why I should have paid attention when the *Chronicle* announced on November 25 that Morris Shepherd, senior senator for Texas, had introduced a congressional amendment to exempt homesteads from taxation on up to five thousand dollars of their value.

Nor would I have known about the circumstances of college students and their plans. The July 15 issue announces a meeting at eight that evening at the county agent's office "of all the boys who are interested in attending Texas A&M," and the August 26 issue reports that eight boys have rented a house at College Station for the coming school term, at sixteen dollars per month. The paper for September 23 announces that the eight have indeed gone off to school, with Mrs. S. A. Munsey accompanying them, to be their house mother. That's long ago and far away: now, often as not, high school seniors have to get their applications in soon after Christmas, and, if accepted, attend diverse kinds of orientation programs long before going to campus full-time.

Down at the Baptist church, according to the *Chronicle*, by November, 1937, Allen Ogletree was the pastor. He was supposed to have saved my soul that time, probably in the summer of 1937, when he baptised me in Credit Lake. At the risk of being a disappointment, sir, I don't much believe that it took. Maybe it was the next summer, and not your fault anyway.

I notice in the July 1 issue that on Sunday, July 4, "the Junior Girls Sunday School Class of the First Baptist Church will have charge of the opening exercises." From the July 15 paper I discover that Peggy Sue Robinson is visiting Orlene and Dennie Branch out at the ranch. I don't know who Orlene and Dennie are, or where the ranch is. The July 12 paper reports that Mr. Poet Hagins died on Monday, July 9, apparently of accidental shotgun wounds to his chest. He was forty. I find in the November 11 issue that Don Jones' parents have a new V-8. In the same paper, W. E. (Med) Wade, Mr. Wade's son, announces that he has disposed of his interest in the Kent Theater, and another notice says that he and his wife have left for Arizona. He was, the report says, "unable to stand the effects of the cotton dust from the Jayton gins which blows over the town about three days out of every week." Nannie Beth Rice visited the dentist at Aspermont, according to the November 25 *Chronicle*, and in the issue for December 9, I found Don Jones' letter to Santa Claus:

> Jayton, Texas, Dec. 3, 1937
> Dear Santa:
>   I want a Northwest Mounted suit, and one pair of boot pants, and all kinds of nuts and fireworks. Please bring me a pair of boxing gloves and a punching bag.
> Joe Donovan Jones

I'm pretty sure he didn't get the Northwest Mounted suit. I think I would have remembered because I would have envied—and might envy still.

The Sans Souci bridge club met through the year. The Coffee

Pot Cafe closed down for a few days in February for some improvement. The issue for February 25 reports that the president is trying to attend to the plight of farm tenants: "More than 60 percent of the farms operated by tenants or croppers are in the ten cotton-producing states," according to the report, and there, it goes on to say, "the condition of the tenants and croppers in those states is more pitiable and their outlook for improving their lot in life is more nearly hopeless." On the same page, Mrs. H. D. May reports that she has planted a hundred Chinese elms on the north and west side of the house to make a windbreak. The March 4 issue gives notice of a city election to be held on April 6. The notice is signed by the mayor. Mr. Wade is the mayor. This appears in the March 18 issue:

> STONEWALL COUNTY LIQUOR STILL TAKEN
> ASPERMONT, March 15—A new 200 gallon whiskey still, 16 gallons of liquor and 2,000 gallons of mash were confiscated late today 15 miles northwest of here by a raiding party led by Sherriff Brooks Ellison of Stonewall County, John W. Coates, district liquor control board supervisor, and his staff from the Abilene headquarters.
>
> Officers expected to make arrests soon in connection with the illicit distillery's operation.

A full-page notice in the same issue announces that April 4 to April 11 is CLEAN-UP WEEK—DO YOUR PART TO MAKE JAYTON "The Cleanest Little City in the West." The ballot printed in the March 25 paper for the forthcoming election shows that Mr. Wade is standing for re-election as mayor. The April 1 paper carries this notice:

> SINGING CONVENTION AT DICKENS, APRIL 4TH
> We extend a hearty invitation for everybody to attend the Dickens Co. Singing Convention at Dickens, Sunday, April 4th.
>   Spread lunch with us and enjoy the day. Good singers will be here; we expect you too.
>   Jack Gipson, President
>   Dickens Co. Singing Convention

The June 17 paper announces a building boom. Among the projects predicted: "The city and county are just waiting to hear from Washington before starting the erection of the City-County office building on the lot owned by the county just south of the *Chronicle* office building. They hope to have this project approved in time to start the work about July 1st." That particular plan didn't work out. No office building ever went up there. I learn from the July 8 paper that "the mineral survey being made of Kent County is bringing to light many possibilities for the utilization of the immense gipsom deposits and deposits of volcanic ash in the county." Peril from grasshoppers (July 15) and from cotton flea hoppers (July 22) is duly noted, and the July 22 paper also reports that the Jayton oil mill is one of the best in the state. The post office closed early on September 30 in order to move to the new location behind the bank. I went there for the Sears Roebuck catalogue; I can't remember where the post office was before.

School News

The notice appeared in the August 5 issue that school would start on September 13. Mr. Coons is by now principal, and the story includes his announcement of the faculty. Among them is Nannie Beth Rice. I guess I was as ready as I was going to get for the second grade. A further reminder of the opening of school appears on September 2.

I haven't told much about Peacock, and know little to tell. Peacock was smaller than Jayton, down the road toward Aspermont, and over in Stonewall County. In the September 23 paper, under the general heading, "Peacock News," this item appears:

School to Close for Cotton Picking

With the end of the week school will close for a period of a month for cotton picking. Mr. Cook stated that he hoped all of the students would start regular attendance when school work starts again. This will help the students as well as the school.

The Weather

The weather was about as chancy as the crops, wherefore the crops were chancy.

On February 10, among the "Personals," this appears: "We don't know which would be the easiest death, that of too much dust in the craw or that of having nothing in the craw. If we knew the latter were less painful we might suggest that the populace of West Texas migrate to some other clime." In a story on terracing and contour plowing in the February 25 issue, Mr. Wade remarks, "Contoured rows have proved quite valuable in the prevention of wind erosion, especially in our loose sand fields. This is especially true in getting a stand on the land since the crooked rows prevent or hamper the movement of the sand down the rows."

Rain did come once in a while. The main headline for March 4 says, "Jayton Territory Gets Needed Rain," and this opening paragraph follows: "Following the late sand storms, wind and more sand storms came the much needed rain that we have been looking and praying for, tho we do not have any idea how much it has rained at the time of this writing." A little later, Mr. Wade continues: "It made us feel that there still is some hope left for the people of this part of West Texas, just to know that when it wants to rain that it can. And too it will do much good to the land and vegetation that has been covered with the dust that has settled over everything since the last duster." In the same issue of the paper, mixed in with the "Personals," is this item: "Somebody ought to get behind a civic improvement club for this town and put Jayton on the map before the dust storms blow it completely off. (How about it?)"

But Mr. Wade reports on April 1 – that territory seldom gets snow even in deepest winter – that a "Three-Inch Snow Supplies Moisture." In the story, he speaks of "the severe sand storms of last week."

I guess the moisture didn't hold. On July 8, this item appears on the front page:

> The weather is hot and dry. While the crops are still doing well, the time is not far in the distance when a rain must be had to keep them growing. The hoppers are pretty bad in some parts of the country, but the farmers are fighting them continually and by the hardest of hard work, are managing to hold them down fairly well.
>
> Reports from Kansas, Nebraska, Colorado and Oklahoma show us that the few hoppers we have in this county would not be noticed in the above mentioned states. At the same time we have enough to do plenty of damage if they are not killed out.

On the second page of the same issue, Mr. Wade remarks that "good showers fell within sight of Jayton Wednesday afternoon but the territory immediately around the town remains very dry." And on the third page, he says local news is scarce – "the hot weather seems to have slowed folks down considerably. . . ." On July 22, rain is reported, following the hottest days of the year. It got hotter. On Thursday, August 5, this story appeared on the front page:

> SOAKING RAIN IS FALLING AS WE GO TO PRESS TONIGHT
> After the hottest day of the year it is now raining and if the rainfall equals the electrical display and comes up halfway to our hopes we will get a good one between now and daylight. At this hour we feel safe in saying a half-inch is assured. But be it little or much it's mighty welcome and badly needed.

This day will perhaps be remembered for years as the day Jayton got the earliest bale of cotton in its history and the night of the day when the two months drouth and a prolonged and withering hot spell was broken.

We hope with this rain there will be plenty of moisture for the putting on of another 2,500 bales of cotton in August and for the filling of cisterns and surface tanks. If it doesn't rain enough tonight for all this it will before it quits. Has it not rained every time this year just when we needed it?

On August 26, another headline says, "Big August Rain Takes Kent County Out of Drouth Stricken Area." The story opens with this: "Since the *Chronicle* was published last week copious rainfall has come to this part of Texas and no longer are we classed as being in the drouth stricken area of Texas. In Jayton the total rainfall was a little better than 4 inches."

But nothing holds. In the last issue of the year (on December 30), this item appears:

Moisture Comes to Kent County This Week
After one of the longest dry spells we have seen or had in many Falls, considerable moisture came to Kent County this week. Foggy, damp weather with the temperatures above normal for this time of the year, brought showers that gradually soaked the ground, and it is all going in for it fell so slow that it did not run off. The wheat fields began showing green at once and winter grasses are putting out and if the warm weather continues it will only be a short time until the winter weeds will become blooming flower gardens and Texas, where the weather is a continual contradiction of itself and nature, may again make of winter an unexpected early spring.

Entertainment and Sports

The *Chronicle* reports on January 21 that the junior class is putting on a show called *The Gay Desperado* down at the Kent Theater. On June 24, notice comes that the Kent is closing:

Jayton Is Again With Out a Picture Show
Again Jayton is without a picture show as Mr. Barnes Purdue has accepted an advertising job with one of the larger chain show companies. It seems as if Jayton just can't get a showman who can put the business over in this town. There are lots of show goers in Jayton but most of them journey to Spur, Rotan, Stamford or Sweetwater or some other distant theater and pass up their home town. They do this not because the out of town shows are better

but just because they like to take to the air and also probably because the old home town needs none of their money while the distant places do. Such is the way of men and women in this day of high powered cars and moonlight nights.

But in the next week's paper, closing has been averted: Med Wade, one of Mr. Wade's sons, has taken over the theater, and Errol Flynn is coming in "Green Light." The July 8 paper announces that a cooling plant is being installed. In the July 29 paper, Med Wade apologizes for the equipment breakdown that caused cancellation of shows and invites folks back to see Richard Arden in "Secret Valley." We learn in the same paper that family admission prices are good only for Friday night and Saturday matinee. On September 9, notice comes that the theater will be open six nights a week, Thursday excepted. The serial that week was "Dick Tracy." On Thursday, November 11, comes the notice I have already mentioned—Med Wade has sold out and is moving to Arizona for his health. In the remaining papers that I have for 1937, I found no advertisements for picture shows.

But other things continue. The March 11 paper summarized the successful basketball season, now over. The girls' team played forty-one games and lost only one, to Peacock, 21–19. The boys' team played forty-three games and lost six. They won their first game of the season 14–6 over Girard, lost their last game by 19 to 7 to Peacock. Between them, the two teams played teams from Girard, Peacock, Swenson, Snyder, Clairemont, Aspermont, Patton Springs, Floydada, Dickens, Spur, Ralls, Goodman, Anson, Avoca, Idalou, Abilene, Merton, Spade, Dumont, Noodle, Rule, Divide, Roscoe, and Talpa.

And more. The March 18 issue announces the forthcoming Texas Interscholastic League contests. I notice that Curtis Hancock and H. J. Whatley—both soon dead in the war—were the boys' high school debaters. Some results were in and given in the April 1 issue; at the time, Girard was leading.

The July 29 issue reports that Jayton's softball team won the tournament in Dickens.

But there's more. Up at Lubbock, I learn in the March 25 issue, "Kent County, as usual, will have a major part in the annual Plains Quality Meat Show." There'll be competition in baby beef, fat pig, fat lamb, and cured meat, and, on March 29, a "supervised fun night is planned for the exhibitors around a huge campfire on the fair grounds." And the June 24 paper says that the Red Hawk program (WFAA and WBAP radio every morning at 6:30 except Saturday, when it's 12:30) has "notified the editor that a special Jayton program will be featured next Wednesday, June the 30th at the morning hour."

And more. The October 7 *Chronicle* says that the Harley Sadler Big Stage Show will be in Jayton on Wednesday, October 13.

And more. The Kent County Fair, held in Jayton on October 8–9, attracted some three thousand people despite rain and muddy roads in the northern part of the county. Where the hell was I? Why don't I remember? A boy, a boy living in the same town, should certainly have been there. Was I? Was I off in the canyons? Why in hell can't I remember something like my first county fair, except of course it wasn't my first county fair if I wasn't there. Prizes were given for quilts, bedspreads, biscuits, and gingerbread, for Boston brown bread and for canned products—beans, peas, carrots, tomatoes, one that I can't read on the microfilm copy, beets, beet pickles, cucumber pickles, peach pickles, pears, peaches, plums, tomato relish, pepper relish, preserves, and jelly. Don Jones's mother won the best bedspread prize—seems incongruous, somehow, since the story was that she could also pick up a hundred-pound sack of feed in her teeth.

And by November 18 they were back to playing basketball. The junior boys' team beat Clairemont 14–7. The players were Tom Bill Fowler, Richard Robinson (that's Red, Peggy Sue's brother), Clyde Goff, Buddy Gallagher, John H. Montgomery, Jimmie Montgomery, Henry Sproules, Tom Wade, and Nolan Corder. That's my big brother. There he was.

THE MARKET REPORT

How strange life is, how odd its connections. In the *Chronicle* for March 18 I come upon an account of sheep-growing in Texas. I gather that Mr. Wade has used it second- or third-hand removed, from the San Angelo newspaper through a publication called *Texas Parade*:

> WOOL A FIGHTING WORD IN WEST TEXAS
> HOUSTON, March 10. —"Wool may be short, but not in Texas," says Sam Ashburn of the *San Angelo Standard-Times* in the March issue of the Texas Good Roads [on this last word, I'm not certain— my microfilm is cloudy] Association's official organ, *Texas Parade*, just from the press.
> "Texans do not hold in dislike the glamour that is woven about the state by novelists, feature story writers and radio artists," writes Mr. Ashburn. "They do, however, at times, become tired of being referred to as a plains state.
> "In the southwest section there are huddled around the hills

and mesas some 8,750,000 sheep, which makes the state a leader
in the production of wool in the United States. . . .

"Wool in West Texas is a fighting word. There is assembled in
San Angelo the greatest inland wool market in the world. . . ."

I read the rest of the story, and I'm still not sure why wool is a fighting
word—is it because West Texans are angry that no one has noticed the
important place they hold in wool production, or is it because of that
old rumored feud between cattlemen and sheepmen?

No matter—I'm more struck by the reference to San Angelo. In
1937, I wouldn't have known where San Angelo was, and, if I had known,
might have shrugged it off as one of those places where sheepmen gather.
In 1987 or 1988, San Angelo matters in quite a different way. I'm writing this on Wednesday, January 27, 1988. Until Friday, my younger
daughter and her husband and their son live there. On Friday, they
will move to Abilene. I have enjoyed their years in San Angelo, have
enjoyed the restaurants Zentner's and Zentner's Daughter, have especially enjoyed walking the grounds of Fort Concho, and still do not
know why wool is a fighting word. I guess it's no great matter after all
this time.

I see by the *Chronicle* for February 10 that Landers and Gardner
Grocery has forty-eight pounds of Light Crust flour for $1.95 (back in
1934, the same amount went for $1.70, and I don't know what the times
are coming to), a no. 2 can of corn for 10 cents, oats, any kind, with
cup and saucer, bowl or plate, for 29 cents, and a bunch of one hundred onion plants for a nickel. Robinson's has a twenty-pound sack meal
for 58 cents and three cans of mackerel for 25 cents. The Jayton Feed
Store advertisement says,

HERE'S HOPING
It turns warm, but if it doesn't, we have the coal to keep the home
fires burning.
We also have feed for the milk cow, hogs and poultry that will
make them produce PROFITS.

Just about every week, the Robinson's advertisement says "EGGS—EGGS—
Bring us your eggs. We pay the highest market price." Twenty-five cents,
most weeks, will get you two pounds of bologna sausage, and on March 4,
forty-eight pounds of flour is down to $1.25. On March 11, Landers and
Gardner is offering two pounds of White Swan coffee for 59 cents, and
18 cents in trade for eggs. That same week, Robinson's says, "Since the
rain we can all smile and work with hopes for the best crop in years,"

offers rice at 35 cents for six pounds, and claims their trade price on eggs is better. Bryant-Link Company offers foundation garments at $1.95 and up, pure silk hose at 69 cents, and tennis shoes for 69 cents.

On April 1, Robinson's warns that prices are going up, offers toilet tissue at six rolls for 23 cents, and announces, "IF YOU HAVE A FAT YEAR-LING, WE WILL BUY IT!" By June 17, Robinson's beats Landers and Gardner on coffee and offers a four-pound bucket for one dollar. That same week, the Bryant-Link Company has "BRASSIERS—Dainty Brassiers of extra good quality, lace and net. Form fitting. All sizes—49 cents to $1.00." On July 8, Landers and Gardner has seven bars of laundry soap for 25 cents and a gallon can of prunes for 33 cents, and Robinson's says, "Yes, the temperature is up and will be up for some weeks but our prices are down and will remain down for all who appreciate quality merchandise." Bryant-Link Company has men's seersucker suits for $4.98.

On July 22, forty-eight pounds of flour is back to $1.69, and you can get twelve bars of laundry soap for 24 cents, three cans of sardines for 25 cents. On July 29, three cans of vienna sausage are available for 25 cents. By August 26, Landers and Gardner has ten pounds of spuds for 17 cents and Post Toasties for ten cents; Robinson's is offering a half-gallon of peanut butter for 55 cents. On September 29, Ivey Murdoch at the Palace Barber Shop says,

> With razor keen and water hot
> You'll always find me on the spot,
> Your hair I'll cut and dress in style
> So the dear girls will return your smile.

On September 9, you can get three cans of potted meat for a dime. On September 23, Bryant-Link Company has new Philco radios for $29.95 and up. On October 21 at Landers and Gardner, a pound of pinto beans is 6 cents. The next week, Bryant-Link has men's union suits at 89 cents a pair. Aladdin Mantle Lamps are available for $4.95. Most folks closed their shops on Armistice Day. On November 18, apples and oranges were a penny each, and coffee is down to 64 cents for three pounds. The Coffee Pot Cafe (yes, it was shaped like a coffee pot), announced,

> The Cleanest and Neatest Place in Jayton
>
> Why Swelter Over a Hot Stove When We Serve the Best of Home Cooked Meals at Depression Prices
>
> The Best of All Good Things to Eat, The Way You Like Them

COFFEE POT CAFE

When in Town, Drop Around

On December 9, at Bryant-Link you could get Daisy Air Rifles for $1.00, $1.75, $2.25, and the pump for $4.50. A single shot 22-caliber Remington was $5.95. A half-gallon of peanut butter is down to 49 cents. One dollar pays for a year's subscription to the *Chronicle*. On December 16, flour is holding and a can of Prince Albert costs 11 cents.

In 1937, I got acquainted with utilities, though I didn't know it at the time. I encountered West Texas Utilities indirectly then, lost the company for close to fifty years, and found it again through my son-in-law, first in San Angelo and now in Abilene.

If I "got acquainted with utilities" or "encountered WTU," that's not exactly the same as being *connected* with WTU. My family was mostly not connected with utilities—only one of the houses we lived in in Jayton (and that only for a short time) had electricity, water, gas, and indoor plumbing. I was generally unaccustomed to such niceties, though I have since learned to love them.

What I first heard about WTU may not have happened, or at least may not have happened as I heard it and later repeated as sure truth. Mr. Huls, down at Huls Drug Store, had a local reputation for the strength of his hands. As I recall him, he didn't *look* as if he'd have unusually strong hands, but according to the stories I heard, local citizens, maybe sitting there for a cup of coffee, loved to introduce strangers to Mr. Huls to see their surprise and then pain at the ferocity of his handshake. Then a new WTU man, Mr. Bradley, came to town to work out of the office on the south side of the square—it's still there, and I met Joy Kidd there.

I wasn't around Mr. Bradley much. He was big, even allowing for a boy's exaggerated recollection, high, wide, deep, and brown from his outside work. Mr. Bradley's wife (I think she and my mother became friends) was given to modern ways and had apparently decided that their son, Don, was not to have tea or coffee until he was grown. I thought he was the worse for that. At any rate, so the story goes, in the course of time the stranger, Mr. Bradley, showed up at Huls Drug Store, and was introduced to Mr. Huls, but this time the Huls handshake didn't work. This time, so the story goes, when Mr. Huls, a small, pale, sedentary man, set out to squeeze the stranger's hand, the stranger, Mr. Bradley, "wrapped a paw as big as a ham" around Mr. Huls's hand, and the Huls magic was broken. I suppose that there's always an outsider who can break the inner barrier, just as sometimes there's an insider who can repel all outsiders.

That was my knowledge of WTU until I read the *Jayton Chronicle*. There's a lot about WTU that I didn't know. There's a lot about *everything* that I didn't know.

Now, reading 1937 in the *Chronicle*, I find WTU again in interesting ways. On July 1, this appears on the first page:

WEST TEXAS UTILITIES SPONSORING CONTEST

The name housewife when applied to modern West Texas women is old fashioned, out of date, and no longer suitable, according to D. C. Bradley [that's strong hand] local manager of the West Texas Utilities Company, who today announced a contest which invites women themselves to select the name they like best.

A little later in the story, Mr. Bradley goes on:

"Greek, Latin, or English may be used," he added. "Just invent a word that describes the modern woman whose talents go beyond the kitchen — the woman who takes an active interest in club and civic affairs, who enjoys some sport such as golf, tennis or even croquet. In fact, invent a name for a woman who is a companion to her family instead of a slave to her kitchen."

In the same issue a WTU advertisement announces the contest with a coupon that must accompany entries. The ad announces

$500 FOR A NAME!
If I'm not a
HOUSEWIFE,
What am I?

Elsewhere in the ad, this appears:

THE MODERN WEST TEXAS WOMAN?
First Prize: Large-sized Frigidaire
Second Prize: Choice of Electric Dishwasher or
washing machine
Third Prize: Sunbeam Mixmaster
Ten prizes of smaller Electric Appliances.

The July 29 issue reports that "Dr. Charles Earle Funk, New York lexicographer and linguist, will judge entries in the West Texas Utilities Company's 'name-a-housewife' contest, Don Bradley, local manager, announced yesterday." The story continues: "Possibility that the name 'housewife' may be omitted from dictionaries of the future was viewed a result of Dr. Funk's participation as judge in the contest." However, as reported in the August 5 issue, Dr. Funk did not seem to think that any new word would receive wide adoption: "Today's public," the item says, "prefers old wines to new wines, old habits to new habits and old lace to new lace but also old words to new words."

The WTU announces on September 2 that Mrs. Ben D. Parker of Abilene ("see photo right") has won the contest. Her proposed new word for housewife? *Neolectress.*

But WTU wasn't through.

A front-page story in the September 23 issue reports a new contest, a $40,000 writing competition on "the electrical standard of living." More WTU news later.

Late-breaking News and Personals

In the October 7 issue, I found my brother again. He was on the junior boys' basketball team that lost to Swenson, 19–5. He must have played the whole game—only five players are listed.

In the October 21 issue, as I reported much earlier, I found myself, though it didn't look like any self I remembered, my little account of the second grade students' train trip to Girard, with my own full name below it.

In the November 4 issue, I found myself again, on the honor roll. Others who made the honor roll were Alva Roy Smith, Jimmy Cox, Olive Engledow, Bobby Elbert Hamilton, Joe Don Jones, Bobbie Nell Fuller, Jimmy Matthews, Lucille Robinson, and Peggy Sue Robinson.

In the December 16 issue, I found myself on the honor roll again. Joe Don Jones didn't make it this time, but Margie Sue Myrick and Billy Glenn Vencil did.

—————— 26 ——————

Nineteen Thirty-eight

We lived for a while on the Lowrance place on the northeast edge of town. Our house was the last in town in that direction. The Croton Breaks began about ten yards from the back door. We had come back from the little house up toward Spur, and I started the second grade in the fall of 1937.

One way to school, the route I took at first, was west along what I still think is a lonesome road that skirts the north edge of town and goes on to the cemetery, though fortunately I turned south well before that. (Later, I learned a friendlier path across the edge of the field in front of the house and curving down through town and past Don Jones's house and on to school.) Then, I didn't know that the lonesome road that ran west past my turn-off and on to the cemetery had a name. I learned only lately that folks call it Cemetery Road. I guess I'm glad I didn't know that then, though I was to learn soon where it went. The *Chronicle* for January 27, 1938, reports that funds have been gathered to buy elm trees for planting on Cemetery Road. On May 5, a notice appears on the front page from Judge Hagins: "Thursday, May 12, is the regular annual Cemetery working day at the Jayton cemetery. Everyone interested is asked to come and bring their dinner and let's give the cemetery a good working and pay our respects to our loved ones who are taking their long sleep in this city of the dead." I've seen tumbleweeds blowing in the dust down Cemetery Road.

Don Jones's grandfather and my Grandpa Corder died at about the same time, and their funerals were on the same day. I still don't know the days of their deaths or the day of their funerals, but the *Chronicle* reports them on Thursday, July 28, the same issue that reports the county's strong support for W. Lee O'Daniel in the primaries:

DEATH TAKES TWO OF JAYTON'S PIONEERS
    Last week-end Death made two calls at Jayton and carried to their final home, two of the pioneers of this part of Texas.
    The first call was made at the home of Mr. J. C. Jones who met death with the same degree of fortitude which had marked his meeting of the problems of life. . . .
    Death's second call was for Mr. R. B. Corder, who had been taken to Abilene, Texas, for surgical treatment. Mr. Corder died after undergoing a major operation from which he never regained consciousness.
    Mr. Corder after coming to this part of Texas lived for a number of years in Stonewall county but for the last 12 to fifteen years had made his home in Jayton.
    He was a clean minded gentleman of the pioneer class. Worked hard and did what he could to care for and educate his family. Honest, with himself and his fellow man. Respected by all who knew him. A faithful church member, he went to his reward without fear and with the hope and the trust of one who has fought a good fight and kept the faith. His departure will be regretted by many and he will be fondly remembered by all who knew him for his true worth as a clean citizen and faithful husband and father.

The same issue carries a note that surprises me, and I don't understand it, and I'm not going to ask my parents about it now. Some things upset them easily these days. The report of the deaths was on Thursday, July 28, but my grandfather's funeral must have been on Monday or Tuesday, and I still don't understand the timing. On the last page of the same issue, this notice appears:

CARD OF THANKS
We wish to express our thanks to the Ideal Security Life Insurance Co., for their prompt payment of Insurance.
MR. AND MRS. N. J. CORDER

I can't ask them now, but I wonder what urged them to thank an insurance company in that particular way. Much about the timing I don't understand, or don't recall: sometime before the funeral, Grandpa was brought in a casket to our house so that friends could pay their respects. I don't know how long his body was there—probably not as long as the stories I've told, but long enough to frighten me. After that, we went to the church, then out along that west-going road to the cemetery. One of my uncles cried. My father didn't cry, but I think he wanted to.

So. I found their note of thanks, but I *didn't* find something else, because most of the following month's issues are missing. My father wrote a poem about his father. Then, I thought it strange that he had taken this way to say his grief. Later, I came to find it less strange. As I remember events, my mother salvaged the scraps of paper he'd written on and took them down to the *Chronicle* office and had the poem printed up nicely on a big card. I believe that Mr. Wade also printed the poem in the *Chronicle*. If he did, it's in one of the issues missing from my file. I'm pretty sure that my mother still has a copy of the poem, but I'm not going to ask her about it right now.

THE NEWS—HARD TIMES, MAYBE

Early in July, in the issue after July 4, Mr. Wade reckoned that these aren't hard times:

HARD TIMES IN TEXAS, NO
Should you hear some one talking hard times in Texas, give them a horse laugh. There is no such thing as hard times in Texas at this time. Now money may be scarce when it comes to buying groceries and the other necessities of life but that's all.

He bases his judgment on attendance at family reunions, Old Settlers' reunions, and especially the Cowboy Reunion and Rodeo held at Stamford over the July 4th weekend. "Enough whiskey and beer was drank," he reports, "to float a battleship," along with "cold drinks of other kinds" and "lake water of various temperatures and grades of purity"—enough, taken together, to "cause an overflow in the Mississippi if it had all been dumped in at one time." On the basis of his calculations, he concludes that "there is no hard times in Texas. Sure some folks bellyache, but there will perhaps be a few achers in or trying to get into heaven."

Still. It looks a little like hard times (and besides, I think Mr. Wade was taking out after waste, not denying hard times). Sheriff's sales show up pretty frequently—I note sales for taxes on July 28 and August 4 and November 24 and December 1, and I probably missed some. The issue for January 20 reports that 364 applications for payment under the Agricultural Conservation Program have been received, and the February 3 issue reports about ten thousand dollars in delinquent taxes for the town.

On March 3, a lead story discusses the new Farm Act and the new cotton quota; the same issue reports that "many farmers are losing their property or undergoing heavy expense to save it, because they fail to take advantage of debt adjustments services offered by the Farm Security Administration," and the next paper urges farmers to study the new Farm Act carefully. The April 21 issue carries an interview with a regional Social Security administrator, in town to try to get all eligible signed up for benefits, and the May 19 issue reports early payments on 1937 cotton, and the June 30 paper announces reduced interest rates on federal land bank loans.

Not hard times, maybe, but not easy. Meanwhile, they're still trying to get Highway 18 hard-surfaced, according to the April 7 paper. The June 30 issue says that work on paving will be started this week, and by October 20, work on the last gap in the highway has begun, that part lying within the city limits of Jayton.

And ominous notes sound. In the issue for March 10, this appears:

PLANES AND PROPAGANDA
With a roar echoed by the shouts of thousands in the streets below, six "flying fortresses," proudest weapon of the U.S. Army, recently zoomed through the muggy heat of Argentine afternoon. Just 36 hours out from Miami, those winged messengers, symbols of America's power in the air, also symbolized America's determination to top alien propaganda in South America.

For months past, Italy, Germany, and Japan have flooded the

Spanish Americas with the cry: "Follow the Fascists!" Wave after wave of radio, press, amusement, and educational propaganda has swept over Latin America, culminating in the trans-Atlantic flight of Bruno Mussolini and his veterans of the Ethiopian "bombing is fun" expedition.

And then, with an ease that left Europe, and Japan gaping, along came the Americans. Zoom: 2,700 miles to Peru. Zoom: 2,500 miles to Buenos Aires. Zoom: back home again. As those "fortresses" roared smoothly over land and sea, America's flying aces won millions of new friends for the U.S. and in so doing showed foreign propagandists that America knows a thing or two about the ancient art of propaganda. . . .

And then, on September 22, this appears:

WHY "PURGE"?
Images of Germany in 1934, Russia in 1937, are conjured by the frequency with which the verb and noun "purge" are appearing in our current American political news. Der Fuehrer had his foes pistoled without trial, and then announced to the world with the felicity for which the German is famous that the country and party had been "purged" of their noxious presence. . . .

Hard times, yes, and hard times coming.

THE STATE OF THE ART IN JOURNALISM

Mr. Wade apparently didn't feel compelled to be eternally objective, and maybe didn't mind echoing himself. On December 15, under the headline, "Local Stores Burglarized Sunday Night," a story began, "Sunday night, while honest men were taking their much needed rest, getting ready for another week of earnest effort to win their bread with sincere and continuous labor, an organization of slimy thieves, unprincipled thugs, lousy loafers, and anything and everything you may feel like calling them, lifted from the safes of five business firms in Kent County, around five hundred dollars in cash, and many valuable papers." Signs indicated that they first went to May's Blacksmith and stole some tools for breaking and entering, then hit the Thos. P. Johnson Dry Good and Ready to Wear, the Bitick-Smith Grocery, and Mayer Auto Service. The other two firms aren't named.

CROPS

When I went back to Jayton thirty years later, or forty years later, the place was far greener than I remembered. Memory is always a little wrong, I expect, but in the March 10 *Chronicle* I found some reason for the later green—Mr. Wade reports that Jayton citizens have set out about five hundred trees this spring.

A summary of 1937 Home Demonstration Agent activities appears in the January 20 issue. Home food supply and kitchen improvement demonstrations dominated the programs for women; clothing and poultry work demonstrations dominated those for girls.

The March 31 paper expects that 1937 conservation checks will be ready soon. The paper is still urging farmers to terrace and to use trench silos. The February 24 issue reports that a serious infestation of grasshoppers is expected for 1938, and the May 26 issue announces that Kent County's supply of grasshopper poison will be ready soon.

In the March 10 paper, Mr. Wade reminds everybody that four dozen eggs will pay for a year's subscription to the *Chronicle*.

On January 6, we learn that pork, once cured, can be stored in cottonseed oil. The oil retards mold growth, we learn, 100 percent, reduces evaporation and shrinkage, and eliminates fly and skipper contamination 100 percent. The meat won't become salty, we're assured, and won't absorb flavors from the oil. The next week's paper carries a warning about trichinosis and urges all to cook pork thoroughly.

A wool loan program is announced on March 31, and the April 14 paper reports that wheat prices have been below parity for the past twelve years.

In the April 21 *Chronicle* the annual commodity report for 1937 appears, an itemized report of food and clothing issued by the Kent County welfare caseworker during the previous year:

Apples, fresh	3,443 lbs.
Eggs	170 doz.
Flour	3,062 lbs.
Grapefruit, fresh	7,570 lbs.
Grapefruit juice	768 lbs.
Meats, canned	2,008 cans
Milk, dry skim	1,026 lbs.
Milk, evaporated	1,821 cans
Oats, rolled	407 lbs.
Onions	1,595 lbs.
Peaches, dried	305 lbs.
Pears, fresh	505 lbs.
Peas, dried	1,476 lbs.
Potatoes	1,700 lbs.

Prunes, dried	1,377 lbs.
Rice, grits	744 lbs.
Vegetables, canned	2,556 cans

In addition, the caseworker distributed 1,468 items of children's clothing, about 630 items of infants' clothing, about 280 of men's and boy's clothing, about 660 of women's and girl's clothing, ten comforters or quilts, six pillow cases, four sheets, and about 1,100 towels. Oil hadn't made everyone rich, though there were still high hopes: the *Chronicle* reports on December 8 that a new strike over in Garza County is giving ten barrels an hour, that five wells are planned in the Stonewell area.

But cotton is the chief concern, most often in the news. On January 27, we learn that cotton is still coming in to the Jayton Bonded Cotton Warehouse, and on February 3 we hear that 10,466 bales of cotton had been ginned by January 16, up 4,700 bales over the year before. The February 24 issue reminds farmers to fill out a work sheet in the county agent's office—purpose of the work sheets being to determine cotton acreage and establish a base for cotton production. In the March 17 issue we hear that up in Washington, Secretary Wallace is urging Congress to enact legislation authorizing immediate disbursement of $130 million in cotton price adjustment payments to those who abide by the cotton program. The March 31 paper is excited about the success of the Jayton Bonded Cotton Warehouse, now housing thirty-three thousand bales of cotton from the area. It's a lot of cotton, all right, when a fellow remembers that an acre won't produce much over a third of a bale. Mr. Wade thinks it's a lot of cotton, too:

> If one man had all this cotton to pick and could handle a bale a week and had started picking on the day Columbus discovered America, he would still have more than 168 years to work before his job was completed. . . . If it was laid down end to end one could walk on cotton from Jayton to Aspermont. It will take more than 1,100 freight cars to haul this cotton out of Jayton to the mills or the coast. If all this cotton was made into kite string, every boy and girl in Texas could have enough string to fly their kite so high in the heavens one could not see them. . . . Folks who have never heard of Jayton before now have cotton stored in Jayton. As long as they live they will remember and talk about Jayton, where they carried their cotton crop in the year 1937–1938 and placed it in a warehouse and secured fair treatment and a reasonable loan on it until it could be disposed of.

A story in the July 14 paper says that Texas has 9,960,000 acres of cotton in cultivation, the least since 1908, and only 78 percent of the

preceding year's acreage. The twelfth bale of the new season is reported in the *Chronicle* for September 1, but by the next week, 175 bales are in. Optimism about the warehouse is down by September 15:

> The continuous hum of the gins of the county tell us plainly that "fall is here" in spite of the fact that the weather says summer is still here, barring a north wind that blew up Tuesday night.
>
> Many fields are white from top to bottom and most of the cotton is being sold as it is ginned because a majority of the farmers are suffering considerable disappointment over the cotton placed in the warehouse last season.

On September 22, Mr. Wade reports that "the Jayton cotton yard had weighed 975 bales of 1938 cotton up until Thursday morning. At this rate the cotton harvest for Kent County will not last very long." Elsewhere in the same issue, he says the cotton crop in Texas "is going to be one big disappointment this year. The crop in many parts of the state is a complete failure." On October 20, however, with 3,000 bales in, he reports that the crop is "even better than expected."

The Weather

Early news is good. The February 17 paper includes this on the front page:

*Two Million Dollar Rain Falls In This Territory
During First Three Days of Week*

Rainfall Between Three and Four Inches:
Breaks All February Records
Starting Monday morning with the lightest of sprinkles which
brought on Monday night's downpour and eased over Tuesday with

97

light showers during the day and night and on Wednesday continued showers with a north wind making it a bit cool and giving this territory a total of more than five inches general rain by Wednesday noon.

And the February 24 issue reports that on Sunday, February 20, a four-inch snow fell. The March 31 paper says that the two days of slow-falling rain on the previous weekend will encourage early planting. Wednesday, April 6, brought everything, as reported in the *Chronicle* for April 7:

BLANKET OF SNOW COVERS WIDE AREA IN WEST TEXAS
Preceded by Sandstorm, Norther and Rain
About the middle of the afternoon Wednesday, one of those things right from the Arctic hit Jayton in the face, and was it a wolf.

At times everything was up in the air from tin tops to telephone poles, and oh, the dirt! If we had owned all the real estate that was on the move and could have nailed it down we would have been a ranch owner instead of a lot claimer.

If the next one is any worse then we would enjoy being a ground hog at times. While the dirt was going up the temperature was going down at a rapid gait.

Before midnight, Wednesday, the gale from the north had attained the fury of a mid-winter blizzard. Rain started falling sometime around 1:00 o'clock which later turned to snow. Thursday morning at 10:00 o'clock approximately 4 inches of snow covered the ground although most of it had gathered in drifts as deep as three feet in some places.

This spell of winter weather was preceded by a couple of days of summer heat. Up until noon Wednesday the populace were in summer attire. Today it's ear mitts, overcoats and over shoes and boots. This is West Texas. Glory Be!

The May 5 *Chronicle* again reports rain, and the June 9 issue reports that the rain has exceeded the need: "There is still time to make crops but what we need now is less floods and more planting weather." On Thursday, June 30, Mr. Wade reports that on Friday, June 24, record-breaking rains (to seven inches) fell in the Jayton trade territory.

Still, bunches of rain at the wrong time don't make the average growing season rainfall any better.

THE NEWS — LOCAL AND PERSONAL

From the January 6 paper I learn that Dr. Alexander, who'd been practising in Jayton for twenty-five years, has moved to Spur. In the next week's paper, I see that Dr. Earl Pearson has located in Jayton, with his office at Huls Drug Store. Maybe for a while there, doctors were hard to keep: in the May 5 paper I see that Dr. Wallace Chiles has decided to locate in Jayton. I don't remember any of the three, but I believe surely Dr. Pearson had already gone—Jayton would have had trouble being sick enough for two doctors, or paying them.

The *Chronicle* for January 6 reports that "Mr. and Mrs. Dee Corder have visited home folks lately." In the January 13 paper I find this:

> MADDUX–RICE
>
> On December 20th, in Kansas City, Mo., Miss Nannie Beth Rice of Jayton and Mr. Chas. W. Maddux of Chicago, Il., were united in marriage. After spending a week in Moberly, Mo., and a week in Chicago, Mrs. Maddux returned to Jayton to resume her work in the Jayton school where she has taught for seven years. She is at present teaching second grade work in the Jayton school. Mrs. Maddux feels obliged to complete her school work here, after which she will join her husband in Chicago.
>
> Mr. Maddux is a designer and holds a responsible position in the city of Chicago. Mrs. Maddux is a general favorite with the school children and is loved and respected by all who know her personally. It goes without saying that she has the sincerest wishes of everyone in Jayton for a happy, useful married life.

But in the cemetery, Nannie Beth, your name is Brown. Who was Mr. Maddux, Nannie Beth, and where did you meet, and who was Mr. Brown, and who were you besides my teacher, and why are you in the cemetery, and how did you come home again? In the next week's paper I notice that Mrs. Charlie Robinson gave a tea for Mrs. Maddux.

The March 10 paper tells that the junior class play, *Good Gracious Grandma*, was a great success. "The Highlight of the play," the paper says, "was the perfect acting of James Wallace Jay who portrayed the part of 'P-Sam,' the negro servant. He was one of the best 'Negro' boys that we have had the pleasure of watching perform on the local stage." I remember P-Sam a little bit, though I didn't see the play, and I don't think I knew his proper name until I saw it in the paper. As I remember my brother's recounting the play, "P-Sam" was the young man's mispronunciation of the Biblical name he had given, "Psalms."

The Baptists had a revival meeting commencing on March 20, so the paper says.

In the June 16 issue, this notice appears:

> ONLY COLORED SUBSCRIBER HAPPY FATHER AGAIN
>
> Monday morning our only colored subscriber, Ed Foster, became the father again and it was an 8 lb. boy. Mother and son

are doing nicely but old Ed, who is just past 67, is stepping about like a two-year-old, but we suspect that it will not be more than a week before Ed will be back down to earth dragging around just like all other folks who are getting close to three score and ten.

Three columns over in the same paper I learn that on the previous Saturday morning Mr. McLam, "Kent County's last old soldier of the Confederate cause, turned in his worn uniform, closed his eyes, and passed to the great beyond."

In the *Chronicle* for June 30 is this: "Mr. and Mrs. Robert Dee Corder of Fort Worth, formerly of Jayton, announce the arrival in their home of Miss Beverly Sue Corder, June 22. The little Miss weighed 8 1/2 pounds. All parties doing nicely." That's my cousin Sue. She's pretty, too.

The revival the Baptists had back in March apparently didn't take. They're at it again in August. I guess it may have been during that revival meeting that I was smitten with what I took to be religion and was baptized down at Credit Lake, but maybe it was back in 1937.

I guess I didn't know until I read the September 1 paper that Cobb Wade, one of Mr. Wade's sons, was the editor and publisher of the *Aspermont Star*. The September 8 issue says that the State Health Department and the Brazos River Conservation Department are about to survey the salt deposits out at Salt Flats, though the purpose isn't known. I see by the September 15 paper that "a cattle truck load of Jayton and Kent County boys" have left for the fall term at A&M, and the October 20 issue says that on Wednesday, October 19, there was a party for Peggy Sue Robinson on her birthday. Hot chocolate and angel food cake were served. Rhoda Lou Kelly was there, and Lucille and Sally Robinson, and Maude Adele Brown, Bobbie Nell Fuller, Janice Jones, Jimmy Matthews, Don Patton, Kenneth Witt, Bobby Elbert Hamilton, Billy Glenn Vencil, and Naylan Vencil, and I'll be damned if it doesn't say that Jimmie Wayne Corder was also present.

The November 10 *Chronicle* carries a story headed "Telegrapher Who Flashed Word of Custer Disaster Dies in Missoula, Montana."

And I see by the December 15 paper that they have just repainted the water tower.

Sports and Entertainment

The big news in 1938 is football, but I'll save that for a little later. The May 19 paper says that the theater is going to open up again around June 1. If it did, it must have closed down again, for the November 3 paper announces that the Kent Theater reopened on Friday, October 28. The September 22 issue says that the Harley Sadler Tent Show is coming on October 3. That may be the time I saw *The Trail of the Lonesome Pine*. That may be the time, and that may be the play. I'm not sure any more.

The basketball season trails off early in the year, and a new season commences late in the year. The January 13 paper tells that Jayton has "played a superior brand of basketball in the tournament here last weekend" to defeat Peacock, 16–12, and win the tournament. Later (on January 27) I learn that the Jayton girls' team has won the county championship. I don't learn much more from the *Chronicle* until November 10, when notice appears that basketball practice begins today.

But the March 24 paper says that the Kent County Track and Field Meet will be held at Clairemont on Saturday, March 26, part of the general county Interscholastic League meet scheduled for March 25 and 26. I should say, by the way, that according to the April 14 paper, Girard won the track and field meet.

Softball was frequently in the news. The April 21 issue announces that Jayton's softball team is playing its first game of the season this very day. (When you talk about basketball, you're talking about the boys at the school; when you talk about softball, that's the men of the town.) Tom Fowler will be the lead-off batter, and Home Run King Skeeter Lewis will also be in the line-up, along with Mr. Coons, the school superintendent, at first base, and the Williams boys and Claude McKenzie and Stinky Davis. The May 5 paper reports that the businessmen of Jayton are trying to organize an official league, and that must have worked: the May 19 paper announces beginning of league play. Harmony has entered a team, as have Rising Star and Peacock, and "the boys from Golden Pond, Center View, Salt Flats, and Clipper" will also get a team together. On May 26, it turns out that there are *four* teams from Jayton—the Pirates, the Tigers, the Giants, and the Yankees. Then I very nearly begin to lose track. By June 9, it appears that there are *two* leagues. One is the Catclaw League, and Jayton has just beaten Girard and McAdoo. Apparently this is the big league of competition with other towns. The community league by now has eleven teams— four from Jayton, others from county communities, a team made up of "the negro workers at the oil mill," and another made up of "the Mexicans in the community." According to the June 16 paper, Clairemont was the early leader in the community league. The June 30 issue tells that Jayton is leading in the Catclaw League, ahead of Girard, Dickens, Spur, Kalgary, and McAdoo.

The Market Report

According to the January 27 paper, down at Landers and Gardner Grocery you could get a ninety-eight-pound sack of flour for $2.95 — that's a little lower than 1937 prices — a twenty-pound sack of meal for 45 cents, a box of Post Toasties for 10 cents, and a pound of jowl meat for 12 cents. Robinson's Funeral Home now has a separate advertisement. Over at Mayer Auto Service, you could get a 1936 Dodge pickup (radio, overload springs) for $485, and 1930 Chevy two-door for $165, a Model A 1929 Coupe for $75. At Robinson's (the store, not the funeral home), a hundred pounds of flour cost $3.30, a quart of sour pickles 18 cents, and apples 10 cents a dozen. At Bryant-Link Company, ladies' shoes were running from $2.95 to $3.95, towels were 16 cents, men's union suits were 69 cents, and Vanette Hose ranged from 89 cents to $1.25.

On July 27, at Robinson's, a half-gallon of mustard was 25 cents, sugar was $1.35 for a twenty-five-pound sack, and a pound of ginger snaps cost a dime. Landers and Gardner has a forty-eight-pound sack of flour for $1.49 (down from $1.95 in 1937), a gallon of prunes for 28 cents, and potted meat for 3 cents a can. Bryant-Link has men's dress shirts ("Nice assortment — Fast Colors") for 98 cents.

On November 10, at Robinson's, you could get a pound of coffee for 19 cents, or a four-pound pail for 81 cents. A forty-eight-pound sack of flour is down to $1.35, still lower than it was a few months earlier. Down at Bryant-Link, they had women's shoes from $1.95 to $3.50, and new hats ("A shipment of Snap Brim Hats in the New Shaggy Felts, Gold, Wine, Black, and Kelley Green").

And WTU was often in the news and had, with other things, one major announcement. The WTU advertisement in the February 17 issue — not the major announcement — says that WTU is now sponsoring Max Bentley in his "Swing Around the World" daily newscast from Station KRBC in Abilene. He will "translate much of the world's news into his own words, thereby giving you a deeper conception" of events. On May 5, this item appears on the front page:

ON THE JOB
When the high winds of Tuesday afternoon blew down several power line poles between Jayton and the city lake, the Abilene headquarters of the company was called and a force was sent here

at once to repair the damage and believe it or not, everything was repaired and power and lights restored to the patrons of the company within a few hours. We call that service worth the money.

The West Texas Utilities Company serves this territory and they never fail to give the patrons of their company value received for their money.

Then, on June 16, the big announcement comes. This item appears on the front page:

Introducing
"Reddy Kilowatt"
With the announcement in today's issue of the Jayton Chronicle introducing "Reddy Kilowatt," D. C. Bradley, local manager

of the West Texas Utilities Company, made this explanation of the new addition to the company's staff.

"For a number of years, we've been seeking some way in which electric service could be pictured to the public. Practically everyone knows about electricity. But to many persons it is a mysterious force which they believe comes out of the sky. In fact, however, it must be generated at a huge voltage then subdued and more or less served on a platter in homes and businesses where it may be safely used at a mere turn of a switch.

"In Reddy Kilowatt we believe we have a figure which illustrates electric service in an unmistakeable manner which immediately suggests electric service. . . ."

Inside the same issue a WTU advertisement appears with the famous but long-gone figure of Reddy Kilowatt.

LATE-BREAKING NEWS AND PERSONALS

I made it on the second-grade honor roll reported in the March 31 issue. So did Jimmy Cox, Olive Engledow, Bobbie Nell Fuller, Bobby Elbert Cox (before, his name was Bobby Elbert Hamilton — I wonder what happened), Don Jones, Jimmy Matthews, Margie Sue Myrick, Lucille Robinson, Peggy Sue Robinson, Cherry Stanley, and Billy Glenn Vencil. A front-page headline on September 8 says, "Jayton School Set to Open Monday," and the story lists the new teachers of the year, foremost among them Miss Sue Kinney of Stamford, who would be my third-grade teacher and the object of my distant love. Sure enough, the next week's issue says that school has opened.

The *Chronicle* for Thursday, October 27, announces that the PTA is sponsoring a carnival on Monday, October 31. The paper further announces that the third grade put on a play, *Cornelius the Crafty*, and the paper still further announces that I was in the play. I'm damned again if I did it. But I did make the honor roll reported in the same issue, and there were fewer of us this time — Don Jones, Lucille Robinson, Peggy Sue Robinson, and me. The November 3 paper reports that I was president of the third grade's Health Club, and I'm damned if I did it.

And then, in the December 8 paper, there is the news that I still can't believe:

THIRD GRADE TO PRESENT PROGRAM DECEMBER 16
The Third Grade of Jayton Public School will present the following play in chapel Friday December 16:

Play—*There's Always a Santa Claus*—by the third grade. The characters are:

Polly—Peggy Sue Robinson
Billy—Jimmy Wayne Corder
Jack Frost—Robert Howell
Doll—Olive Engledow
Mother Goose—Leona Boling
Holly Wreath—Don Patton
Man in the Christmas Poem—Bobby Elbert Hamilton (he's back
    to Hamilton again, not Cox)
Christmas Star—Billy Glenn Vencil

The rest of the program for that day will be:

Reading—"Mrs. Santa Claus"—Bobbie Nell Fuller
Reading—"A Greeting"—Hanford Long
Song—"Christmas Bells"—by entire third grade

I have no recollection of the event, or of some of the people involved. I will not testify that I was there.

But I did make it on the honor roll again, witness the December 15 *Chronicle*: I'm there, with Don Jones, Bobbie Nell Fuller, Lucille Robinson, and Peggy Sue Robinson.

— 27 —

The Heroes Have Gone from the Grocery Store

Years later—just now—I came through curious circumstances to wonder what happened to my baseball scrapbook of 1937, or maybe 1938, or maybe 1939. This interest began in a series of sorry events in my freshman English class last fall. You have to understand that for close on ten years I have been writing the essays that I assign to my students, turning mine over to them as they turn theirs in to me.

I'd like to believe that what happened was in an appropriate context for the class. That, I suppose, is of no great moment to anyone else, but matters considerably to me. At any rate, one morning in class I was playing my cello real hard, telling them that there was no such thing as a dull subject if you cared about yourself. They reacted predictably enough, thought up four or five dull subjects, selected the one they thought was the worst, and challenged me to write my next essay on their dull subject. Their dull subject? A single Cheerio.

I put off writing the essay for a while, pretending that I was thinking it through. Finally, I went to the grocery store just off campus, bought a box of Cheerios, and set out to work my way down to a single Cheerio. I studied the box and its insides, counted the Cheerios (there are about twenty-six hundred, for the cynical among us), and selected the one I'd write about. But that's not part of my story. My story, for present purposes, starts from what I saw when I studied the outside of the Cheerios box.

Though I mostly believe in a breakfast made of pipe tobacco and coffee, I have spent my time, as three children grew up, in front of the grocery shelves where cereals are displayed. Selecting a cereal is not a casual art, and I have studied the craft, or so I thought.

My own pretensions to expertise notwithstanding, the Cheerios box brought me up short. (I want to report, before I go on, that I was able finally to write a wonderfully adequate essay about a single Cheerio.) What was on the outside of the box troubled me. Perhaps I'd never looked as closely as I had thought. Perhaps I hadn't paid enough attention over the years. What was there? The Hugga Bunch Kids— Hugsy and Impkins and Bubbles and Chumley and Huggins and Hug-a-bye ("Free inside two Hugga Bunch Easy-Paint Postcards").

I cannot account for what happened next. Perhaps it was a simple sequence of associations. Perhaps it wasn't simple. When you go back in time looking for something like the truth, sooner or later you come to abut the place of which there is no knowledge, whether that is prior to birth, in inadequate records, in mistaken memory, or elsewhere. You come to abut that place in any search, I've already suggested, if you go *back* in time, if you go *out* toward others, if you go *sideways* into your self in other manifestations or as perceived by others, if you go *down* into the subconscious, if you go *up* to wherever.

So, I don't know how to account for what happened next. When I saw the Hugga Bunch Kids on the Cheerios box, my mind went to Dizzy Dean and a Wheaties box, to the school year of 1937–38 or 1938– 39, when I was in the second grade or maybe the third grade and started my baseball scrapbook, to the series that ran on the Wheaties boxes, "My Greatest Day in Sports." No trail of bread crumbs can be counted on to get you from the Hugga Bunch Kids to Dizzy Dean, but such transferences do occur.

As I recall that particular series on the Wheaties boxes, it was a continuing account, by diverse sports figures, of their most thrilling day in sports. Charley Gehringer, the greatest second baseman of all, was also in the series, but it was Dizzy Dean who came to my mind, recalling as his greatest day the last game of the 1934 World Series, when the

Cardinals beat the Detroit Tigers, 11–0, to take the championship. I cut out the story and picture for my scrapbook.

Suddenly, that day, I was startled by the change, on the back of cereal boxes, from Dizzy Dean to the Hugga Bunch Kids—Hugsy and Impkins and Bubbles and Chumley and Huggins and Hug-a-bye. Dizzy would have thrown up.

So, startled, I did what I thought a scholar ought to do. I quit grading papers, quit doing whatever I was supposed to do, and went in search of information about this great cultural shift, from Dizzy Dean to the Hugga Bunch Kids. I set out to find traces of Dizzy Dean and all of the athletes who used to be on cereal boxes. I went looking for Wheaties boxes.

The library yielded James Gray's *Business Without Boundary, the Story of General Mills.* The first run of Wheaties was ready for the market in November, 1924. Early on, Donald Davis insisted that the Washburn Crosby Company (as the company was then known) learn to use the new medium, radio, and by 1926, the first singing commercial was ready:

Have you tried Wheaties?
They're whole wheat with all of the bran.
Won't you try Wheaties?
For wheat is the best food of man.

After expanding sales with two radio programs, first "Skippy," then "Jack Armstrong," the company turned to a larger audience, began to sponsor baseball games on radio, and through Knox Reeves, one of the company's advertising agents, found its magic phrase, "Breakfast of Champions." Sales tripled during the depressed 1930s.

That's okay, so far, I thought, but still no Dizzy Dean, no series called "My Greatest Day in Sports." I wrote to General Mills. A pleasant correspondence with Jean Toll, corporate archivist, followed. She was pleasant. What she taught me wasn't pleasant.

Her letter of April 28, 1987, brought me photocopies of various Wheaties package *fronts*, 1924–76. Her letter of July 8, 1987, brought me word that she could not find the series I had asked about; with it were photocopies of two Wheaties *backs*, one from 1935 showing Dizzy Dean and his brother Daffy, hunkered down, examining a baseball, one from 1937 showing Joe DiMaggio stretched high to take a long fly, with the testimony, "Wheaties is just about the swellest dish I've ever eaten. A World Series thrill in breakfast enjoyment." Neither picture was accompanied by other text; there was no account of that 11–0 final game of the 1934 World Series. Her letter of August 5, 1987, brought more photocopies: from 1934, Jimmy Foxx, Ellsworth Vines, Jack Armstrong of Hudson High, Lou Gehrig, Chuck Klein, Mickey Cochran, Betty Fairfield—a golfer, Pepper Martin, Elinor Smith—a flier, Al Simmons, Wally Berger; from 1935, Bill Dickey, George Barclay, All-American guard from North Carolina, and the *Normandie*; from 1936, Jack Knaby, a flier, and Pepper Martin again.

"My Greatest Day in Sports" did not appear anywhere. There was no picture of Dizzy Dean with an account of that game, no picture of Charley Gehringer with an account of his greatest day. Ms. Toll said there had been no such series on Wheaties boxes.

I can still remember cutting out the back of that Wheaties box to put it in my scrapbook. Apparently, the box I remember never existed.

Some time passed in depression before I could go on. Then I tried again. I didn't *always* eat Wheaties. From time to time I tried other cereals in those days. On July 29, 1987, I wrote to General Foods, thinking maybe the box and picture and text I remembered had been on Grape Nuts Flakes, or maybe Post Bran Flakes, or maybe even Post Toasties, though God knows they turned soggy the moment you put milk on them. I've had no answer from General Foods. I don't believe they're going to write.

I mostly know what's on the cereal boxes now, but I can't find Dizzy Dean and the text of that 1934 most thrilling day. Wheaties has Chris Evert (the large box has Walter Payton). Total has Angela Lansbury's Mystery Sweepstakes, featuring the "Mystery of the Missing Vitamins." Captain Crunch has the captain and a bunch of kids marveling over the spinning globes to be found inside the box. Shredded Wheat has a wonderful diagram of a wheat kernel and a recipe. Trix has a connect-the-dots puzzle called "Who gummed up the Trix machine?" Fruit Loops has a color-by-number picture of protoceratops. Corn Chex, for God's sake, has instructions about how kids can fly free on Piedmont. Cocoa Pebbles has instructions about how to get private eye glasses like Fred Flintstone and Barney Rubble wear. I can't go on. I mostly know what's on the boxes now.

But I can't find Dizzy's text. These days, it's hard to find a text under any circumstances. Does it exist on the page or in the speech? Does it exist only in a reader's or a hearer's interpretation? Do I grow fuzzy around the edges and blur before your eyes? Do I disappear even while I speak, as you interpret—or ignore—what I say? Have I gone altogether? I know that Dizzy Dean did, in fact, pitch a six-hit shutout that time in the 1934 World Series, that the game was never in doubt after the third inning. But I can't find the Wheaties box, or his text. Perhaps it's no matter. Ole Diz didn't write it, anyway.

The catch is, I *thought* he did. The catch is, I *thought* I had a text of sports. It came from John Tunis and from piles of pulp magazines. It came from Ralph Henry Barbour and all those books about the wonderful lads at Yardley High and from Wheaties boxes. It came from Jayton, where I grew part way up—and I didn't even get that part right. For years, I've told my children and anyone else who would listen about my brave older brother, and how he was a starting guard when he was just a 135-pound sophomore.

He wasn't. I learn latterly, from Mr. Parker's microfilmed newspaper in Jayton, that he was a substitute, just a substitute. And my sports text came, too, from Texas Christian University, in 1938, when the TCU Horned Frogs were national champions and Davey O'Brien and Ki Aldrich were more than a boy could imagine. I first learned about universities by listening to Saturday afternoon games in 1938, the first year I was much acquainted with radios. TCU beat Centenary, 13-10, then

Arkansas, 21-14. Then they played Temple and won 28-6. Next was A&M, and the headline said, "Frogs Smash Aggies, 34-6! Aldrich, O'Brien Star." Then they beat Marquette, 21-0, and Baylor, 39-7, and Tulsa, 21-0. The headline on Sunday, November 12, said, "O'Brien's Passes Sink Texas, 28-6." Then they won over Rice by 29 to 7. Finally, the headline for November 26 said, "Frogs Use Power to Beat Ponies, 20-7, for Conference Title." A little later, they played Carnegie Tech in the Sugar Bowl and won 15-7.

The catch is, I *thought* Dizzy Dean wrote that text that I can't find. The catch is, I thought the lads all went out for football *after* they arrived at the University. The catch is, I thought I had a sports text. I kept telling myself stories. Peter Brooks remarks in *Reading for the Plot* that "our lives are ceaselessly intertwined with narrative, with the stories that we tell and hear told, those we dream or imagine or would like to tell, all of which are reworked in that story of our own lives that we narrate to ourselves in an episodic, sometimes semiconscious, but virtually uninterrupted monologue." I told myself stories, and thought I had a sports text.

But much that I saw and thought, I saw and thought wrong, and then misremembered. Most things, I never saw at all. I took as mine a vision that is or was, as Garry Wills put it in *Reagan's America*, "beyond or below ideology," a vision that comes from America's past, but doesn't reflect reality at all. Parts of it never did, and other parts no longer do. Reluctant as I am to call up such a company, I've joined the fellow in the White House and thousands of my countrymen in what I didn't yet know was pretense and self-deception, mistakenly enacting again a peculiarly American form of the idea of innocence, invoking again and again, as Stanley Hoffman put it in his review of Wills's book (*New York Review of Books*, May 28, 1987, p. 6): "the cult of the individual acting without any need for historical process, social transaction, political pressures, the play of interests, and myth of the small town as the locus of purity and simplicity, the celebration of sports as a moral paradigm for the young, where innocence and aspiration verge on the religious, the conviction that evil can only come from the outside. . . ."

These myths, I come lately to find, may only be defense against some reality that I haven't been able to deal with—say the reality of my own mistakenness, or the reality of a capitalism and a technology that render the individual powerless, except if he is a thief or a terrorist or a lawyer or a Wall Street broker.

You see, I thought it was all the way it is in Roy Stokes's book,

Andy at Yale, published in 1914. I thought pitchers were pure and intense. I thought the lads went out for football *after* they arrived at the university.

My sports text was wrong. I didn't get most of it right the first time, and then I misremembered what I had misunderstood. Now it's gone. I can't find the Wheaties box that I was looking for. My sports text won't re-create itself, and I've come to know that if your heroes aren't regenerative, you're lonesome when they die.

Some time ago I read in the newspaper that Ken Maynard had died. The news brought on another considerable depression. I felt so low that I had to refrain from grading papers. Lou Gehrig was long since dead. Babe Ruth was long since dead, and so was Honus Wagner, and so was Tris Speaker, and so was Christy Mathewson. Franklin D. Roosevelt was long since dead, and when you get to be fifteen before you realize that anyone else can be president, then the rest sort of seem like imposters. And now, the last of the Big Five was dead.

Tom Mix died in 1940 in a car wreck. Buck Jones died in 1942 in the terrible fire at the Coconut Grove. Hoot Gibson died in 1966 of cancer. I don't know what happened to Hopalong Cassidy, but he's gone. And now Ken Maynard was dead at seventy-seven. He made three hundred western movies and sometimes in the 1930s earned as much as eight thousand dollars a week. But he died in a small house trailer, alone, of physical deterioration and malnutrition. And all those others died, and the list is long, so long.

If your household gods are not regenerative, then you're lonesome when they die, or depart. The heroes have gone from the grocery store, and we are left alone, a very small remnant, studying to be freed from arrogance, hoping to be let loose from ignorance, wanting to be saved from dogma and mistaken memory, alone, trying to figure out how in the world to be heroic ourselves.

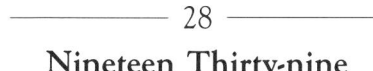

28

Nineteen Thirty-nine

We still have sandstorms in the territory where I live, of course, though not as frequently as in those days, and when they do come, they're mostly not as fierce and grating. I don't suppose I'll ever understand altogether how, when a sandstorm comes down out of the northwest, I can be

at once afraid and worried, hating old images that haunt me, *and* ex-
hilarated.

Not long ago, I sat looking out of my office window toward the
northwest and west, where God lives on top of the Double Mountains.
I was watching a sandstorm. I couldn't see the Double Mountains. They
are too far, five hours of driving, supposing I could get away. I couldn't
see God, then or now. He (or She, as the case may be) is too far, maybe
ten billion miles, or on top of the Double Mountains, or all the way
next door. She (or He, as the case may be) might be just across the way.
I couldn't see just across the way from my window. I could see the near-
est buildings on campus and the first row of live oaks. Beyond that,
the sandstorm, the horizon gone, the world all one color.

But when I went outside, the old thrill was there for a moment,
as when God rides down out of the west northwest on a hard blue
norther, or rides the whirlwind, rides the sandstorm down the Cap Rock.
Outside, I could see one small stretch farther, the stadium outlined
against the dust, a second stand of trees scarcely sketched. I heaved and
breathed gladly for a moment, felt God for a moment in the wind and
plenty of life, but could not see house, home, horizon, high, far, or God.

A story in the *Chronicle* for February 15 seemed to catch, not the time and place that was, but the time and place that I have so often remembered, sometimes incorrectly:

> Drifting Men Mean Drifting Soil, FSA Tells Land Owners
> "Drifting men mean drifting soil," said A. A. McKinney, Kent County Farm Security Administration supervisor today as he invited land owners of the county to consider using the "flexible farm lease," description of which may be had at his office.
> "This lease provides a method and an incentive," Mr. McKinney stated, "whereby tenants will remain on their land owners' farms for a longer period instead of moving every year.
> "Men who own the soil are the ones most vitally concerned in bringing about improvements encouraging tenants to remain and to take care of the land as if it were their own," he said in appealing to landlords to consider the flexible lease and other current proposals to improve tenancy conditions.
> "The foundations of agriculture in this state are threatened by difficulties within the cotton industry," Mr. McKinney continued, "and it is imperative that we develop a system depending more largely upon livestock and other diversified farm products. This cannot be done with farmers who stay upon a place for only one or two years. They must have time to build up their herds, develop pastures, build barns and fences.
> "It is not the purpose of the flexible lease," he explained, "to benefit either land owner or tenant at the expense of the other. But it would stimulate mutual benefits, such as we already find in this very county, where some tenants have remained for a number of years and have planted orchards, built terraces and new buildings and improved old ones. Tenants of this type would multiply many times if assured that they will remain upon the land until they have received benefits of their labor and expense, or that they will be fairly repaid for these improvements in case they should be required to move through no fault of their own."

Drifting men, drifting soil. My family never owned land; we were never upon the land, but what happened on the land determined my father's work.

Before 1939 ended, my family would be gone from Jayton.

The News

I see by the paper on January 5 that paving is complete through Jayton and that now they're expecting a paved road west across the Salt Fork of the Brazos. The July 20 issue says that contracts will be let in late fall, news that's echoed in the August 31 paper.

The issue for March 2 announces that Saturday, March 4, is Trades

Day. I still don't understand why I didn't know something was going on downtown on the first Saturday of the month. Did I stay in my own backyard? Go to the canyons? Go downtown and not notice anything? See everything and not remember? The June 1 paper says that what's now called First Saturday on June 3 will be a humdinger with rodeo events, barrel racing, pole climbing, and other notable activities. Why did that not get into my mind? Or, if it got into my mind, why did it all go out again? The June 8 paper reports that the day was a great success, says, further, that Don Jones was a contestant in the barrel race. The issue for July 6 reports another successful First Saturday, July 1; Uncle Dave Winters, "coming 93," won first, second, and third prizes in the "Old Fiddlers Contest." The paper on October 12 reports another good First Saturday. I wonder where the hell I was.

Sheriff's sales continue. I don't know that I caught them all in the paper.

And the news goes on. The January 5 *Chronicle* announces that the new county officials took office on Monday, January 2. The February 2 paper carries a story out of Austin urging people to be vaccinated for smallpox. New work sheets are ready for cotton farmers according to the February 8 paper, and the March 23 paper reminds all that April 15 is the last day to sign work sheets. On February 27, according to the *Chronicle* for February 22, farmers are invited to meet up at the school auditorium for the purpose of forming a county agricultural association.

On March 23, it looks like Mr. Wade is up for mayor again in the election to be held on April 4. Mayor Wade announces clean-up week in the March 30 paper, and in the April 6 paper, results of the election are given. Continuing Mayor Wade got ninety votes, L. H. Mason got nine, J. W. Barfoot got two, A. J. Suits got three, Howard Johnston got two, and Glen Huls got one. In the same paper, I see that Mrs. Lula Balch presented an interesting discussion of the trend of art and culture during the Renaissance at a meeting of the Jayton Culture Club. The June 1 issue tells me that the woodwork of the Barfoot Hotel is getting a new coat of paint this week.

On June 8, Mr. Wade is speculating that little businesses are doomed to die. As an example of the problem, he says, "Let's bring it right down to the farm":

> Can a little farmer with only one mule and a Georgia stock
> raise cotton in competition with his neighbor who is able to buy
> a four row tractor outfit and cultivate two sections while the little

man is cultivating ten acres? If the little man had to borrow the money to operate on it would cost him at least 12 per cent, whereas the big fellow could get all he needed at 5. More than ever, we're convinced that the fellow that has, gets, while the fellow who has not, gets GOT. No wonder so many are on government relief and so many more are headed directly that way.

They began surveying farms on June 19 to determine crop allotments, so the June 22 paper reports, and the June 29 paper reports that $65,212.47 in conservation checks had been received in the county. On August 17, Mayor Wade through Publisher Wade announced "WAR DECLARED: Tin Cans and Trash Must Be Cleaned Out of Jayton," and I learn from the August 31 paper that the first cotton parity checks have come in. More checks are reported on September 14. A story out of Cleveland in the October 12 paper cites Dr. Antonio Longoria, wealthy Cleveland scientist, who claims to have invented a death ray and later destroyed it, and "who said today that death rays may strike down millions if the European war continues."

A Little Journalistic Note

Mr. Wade's obituaries sometimes moved to an old-time rhythm, as the August 31 paper illustrates: "Monday, August 28 at 2:15 o'clock p.m. Mr. J. H. Deaver drew his last earthly sigh and passed over the river to the city of everlasting life."

The News — Crops

The January 5 *Chronicle* recommends frame gardens, and a story on January 19 advocates trench silos again. Approval of new water facilities programs, announced by Secretary of Agriculture Wallace and reported in the February 2 issue, includes the Duck Creek and Croton watersheds, and makes federal assistance available for construction of ponds, reservoirs, wells, spreaders, springs, dams, windmills, and stock tanks.

The May 25 issue announces "An Epochal Event in the History of Texas Agriculture," the passing of the State Soil Conservation Act providing for "organization of conservation districts based on watershed areas, control by farmers from local to state set-ups and close co-operation with the federal soil conservation service in actual work." A bare note on the front page of the July 13 paper says, "On account of

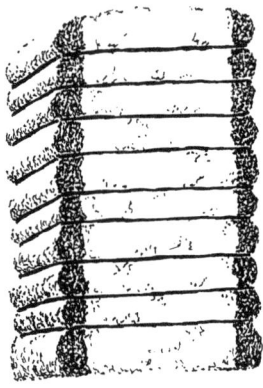

the dry weather during the winter and spring, Kent County failed to have a wheat harvest this year." The September 28 paper reports that the Duck Creek soil conservation district has been approved; the district involves Dickens, Kent, and Stonewall counties. The same issue says that cattle feeders were in the county this week buying up choice whiteface cattle to take to Iowa feed lots.

The February 2 paper announces that 8,311 bales of cotton were ginned in Kent County from the crop of 1939, prior to January 16, as compared with 10,466 bales for the crop of 1938. The *Chronicle* for April 27 informs me that "an average ton of cottonseed yields approximately 311 pounds of crude oil, 906 pounds of cake or meal, 520 pounds of hulls and 143 pounds of linters." The first bale of the next crop, ginned on Tuesday, August 22, 1939, is announced in the August 24 paper, and the September 14 issue expects that one hundred bales will have been ginned by the time the paper is out.

The Weather

Maybe this tells about the weather. In the *Chronicle* for October 19, this item appears: "Jimmie Johnson, Jr. answered the query, 'I have about three bales out. Yea, out yonder in the sand scattered over about three sections.'"

Good rain came in early January. By March 2, however, this notice is on the front page:

FIRST SPRING SANDSTORM HITS JAYTON MONDAY

Monday Jayton enjoyed her first real sandy of the season. The wind began drifting the dust particles about 10:00 a.m. and by 2:00 p.m. the sand was rolling and by 5:00 p.m. tin cans, pebbles, loose planks, anything and everything that was not nailed down was in the air. Hit and miss, tearing across the country like a mad bull that had foolishly knocked down a hornet's nest. But in time the wind wore itself out and Tuesday morning came in bright and calm and if you were not on hand the evening before you would doubt such a thing as a sandstorm ever had been playing around in your back yard.

Two weeks later, on March 16, this appeared:

THIS WEEK'S SECOND SANDY REACHED JAYTON TUESDAY

Well folks, Jayton caught another one of those things called sand storm Tuesday evening. While it threatened all day, the varmint did not exactly stick his nose into town until exactly six o'clock. It soon developed into an old "HE" with whiskers on his chest, dust, sand and grit in his craw that made us old-timers sorter talk timid when facing him and cuss like troopers when we took time out to turn our backs.

But this Wednesday noon it is as lovely as a day in June, tho not quite so warm, and if one did not know better what happened yesterday evening and last night, would not seem possible.

But we learn on April 6 that a good one- to two-inch rain has come, and the May 18 papers says, "Long Drouth Broken by General Rains Over West Texas."

Water, nevertheless, is not abundant. The June 8 paper reports that the well equipment out at the City Lake broke down and they had to pump water into the town main from the pump on the square, but after twenty hours that pump gave out, so they took the fire truck over to Credit Lake, where water had always been free (and pretty dirty) in bad times, and used the fire hose and pump to get water into the pipes again. The next week's paper reports that the pump on the square has been repaired, but two notices on the front page, one from Mr. Wade, the other from the fire marshall, urge sparing use of water. The fire marshall says, "Let's all be careful and not drain the water tank on the City Water Tower," and continues:

Watch the Black mark. When it is at the bottom the tank is full, as it goes up the water does down. When the black mark is in the middle the tank is half full. We must keep enough water on hand to protect us against fire.

> Use water sparingly when the black mark is above the middle
> of the tank.

When they were drinking from the city tank or from Credit Lake, they
were drinking gyp water, which tastes wonderful when it is cold and
is marvelously antithetical to constipation. The next week's paper (for
June 22) reports that they are now able to start pumping again from
City Lake, that the lake has had a good new supply of rain water, that
there will be "No More GYP After Next Tuesday." Later, on September
21, this word comes:

> DRY SEPTEMBER OF NO BENEFIT TO FARMERS
> For the first time in 19 years September has failed to bring rain
> to this territory. So far twenty days have come and gone and not
> so much as a dust laying shower has fallen to relieve the burning
> crops and parching grass. As a rule, in fact as far back as we are
> personally acquainted with this part of Texas it has always rained
> between the first and 20th of this month to make the sowing of
> fall grains possible and start the fall grasses growing, but not this
> time.

And then on September 28, Mr. Wade says we're in for drought as bad
as there's been: "Not a drop of rain in this territory for the past 60 days
and the way it looks now it never intends to rain again." Rain doesn't
come until October 8. By that time, I guess, my father was already hunting for work elsewhere.

NOT EXACTLY NEWS

In the July 20 paper, Mr. Wade ran an article that had originally
appeared in the *Fort Worth Star-Telegram*, headed "Salt Lake in Kent Is
Texas Beauty Spot":

> Approximately 100 tons of almost pure salt are being surface
> mined annually from Kent County's famed 540-acre Salt Lake, lo-
> cated eight miles northeast of Jayton.
> The lake, fed by salt springs, has been the undisputed source
> of salt supplies for over 500 years, Indian inscriptions say.
> Located in the half-mile-deep sanctuary of Croton Breaks, Salt
> Lake was first used by buffalo hunters from 1874 to 1878 as a salt
> supply source and later by pioneer settlers of Kent, Stonewall, Fisher
> and Scurry Counties.
> Men like "Uncle" Alec Shipp of Harmony, Judge Allen, Roby,
> Orvil Lowrance of Jayton and W. V. Jones of Camp Springs recall
> vividly how early settlers in the four-county area used to take sev-

eral days off when work was slack to load up with supplies from the Salt Lake for stock, meat curing, and household use.

The article goes on to tell how game trails lead to the Salt Lake, and how Coronado passed by. My father remembers going with his father in a wagon to get salt for home use. The sesquicentennial edition of the *Texas Almanac* lists under *recreation* for Kent County, "Hunting, local events; scenic croton breaks and salt flat." I've never been to the "Salt Lake" mentioned in the article. I've been along Croton Creek, seen startlingly white salt deposits in the bed and along the sides, but have never been to the place they call "Salt Lake," have been in the vicinity, have been blocked by fences and my own timidity.

The News—Local and Personal

In the *Chronicle* for April 13, this item appears on the front page:

> Once upon a time we went to church where they were holding a revival meeting. After the preacher had delivered a hair raising discourse on the horrors of hell and the home of the damned, and the choir was singing a call for the sinners to come home, the preacher came down the aisle and stopped with his hand on the shoulder of the man who was sitting on the bench by our side. Leaning over, the preacher said, "Brother, are you religious?" The reply was "How can I be religious when I have no flour in my house?"
>
> A hungry nation is the same as a hungry man, only much more dangerous.

But back to January. The January 5 issue reports that local college students have returned to school after the Christmas holiday; Pete Lane, Joe Dick Lewis, Milton Sandell, Euell Harrison, H. J. Whatley, George Rice, Harvey and John Robinson, L. H. Matthews, and Curtis Hancock all went back to Texas A&M; Lucille Daniels and Wynelle McKenzie went back to John Tarleton; Richard and Katherine Jay and W. J. Garrett went back to McMurry; Lee McLaury went back to West Texas State Teachers College at Canyon.

From the January 19 paper I learned that Richard Jay "played the game of his life" in McMurry's basketball loss to Abilene Christian College.

The February 15 paper announces the *Chronicle*'s misspelled word contest, with a total of six dollars in prizes and twenty tickets to the Kent Theater: "There is no catch to the Misspelled Word Contest. The contest is open to all readers of the *Chronicle* except employees of the *Chronicle* and their immediate families. There is no drawing or any element of chance. Whether or not you win a prize depends on your ability in finding the mispelled words. Simply list any misspelled word you find anywhere on the Spelling Contest page, together with the name of the firm in whose advertisement the misspelled word was found." The same issue, in a full-page advertisement, offers forty-five weeks of the *Chronicle* for forty-five eggs.

The March 2 issue tells me that Gardner and Landers Grocery is now just Gardner's, and the March 30 issue says that the Baptists are at it again, with a revival to begin on April 9. The same issue reports that "for the first time in years track meet in Kent County failed to bring on a sandstorm," and that Tom Wade won first in junior declamation, Nolan Corder second, in the county meet. The April 13 paper says that Dr. A. J. McElroy has located in Jayton and will practise medicine there, with his office at Huls Drug. I learn in the same issue that Heb Wade, who has been working in the "mechanical department" at the *Chronicle*, has taken a similar job at O'Donnel in the printery there. "Heb is qualified to do good work in all departments of a country shop front or back."

"Nellie Sue Durham of the Spur Sanitarium visited her sister Mrs. Nolan Corder last week end," the May 11 paper tells me, and the May 25 paper says that Sue Kinney returned to her home Sunday afternoon. I guess school was over, and my teacher went back to wherever. She was back soon, though; the July 20 paper announces that "Miss Sue Kinney, teacher in the Jayton Public School in Jayton, was seeing friends and tending to business in Jayton Tuesday of this week."

An intriguing item appears on July 6:

DOCTOR CHARGED IN SLAYING DIES

ASPERMONT, July 5—Dr. D. C. Wyley, 45, under a charge of murder in the fatal shooting of Dr. D. L. Dodd, 41, his former office partner, died in a Stamford hospital at 7 this evening.

Dr. Dodd was shot to death in a drug store here last Friday night and soon afterward Dr. Wyley was found at his home with a bullet wound in his left side. He was taken to Stamford where he later developed pneumonia.

Funeral for Dr. Dodd was held Monday. Arrangements for the Wyley funeral were incomplete tonight.

Association of the two men began about 10 years ago when Wyley was a student, Dodd an instructor at Baylor Medical College in Dallas.

The September 21 issue reports that J. W. Smith of the Golden Pond community is selling chairs, stools, small tables, and small chests made of mesquite. The same paper has an advertisement for the Green Castle Cafe, which apparently was located where nothing should have been.

The September 28 paper says that the Peacock school let out for a month on Friday, September 22. The principal reckoned that if the weather continued to be fair, maybe the cotton crop could be gathered in less than a month. In the same paper, I see this: "Carry home a sack of hot delicious hamburgers, 3 for 25 cents. Green Castle Cafe." From the October 12 paper, I learn that the Coffee Pot Cafe is open under new management.

The October 19 *Chronicle* indicates that, largely through the efforts of P. D. McKinney, local depot agent, who got others interested and found a band teacher, Mr. Fagan, over in Rule, Jayton is to have a school and municipal band. Mr. Fagan, the report says, has already lined up thirty-one students up at the school. The next week's paper says band practice will begin on Monday, November 1. In the same issue, I see that Dr. B. B. Goldman has located in Jayton to take up his practice. Notice is given that Mrs. A. L. McElroy, R.N., will assist him. That's the name of the former doctor. I wonder what happened. I wonder if anyone knows. I wonder if I'll ever have time and energy enough simultaneously to ask.

According to the December 29 paper, the same students who went back to school in January are now home again for the Christmas holiday.

Sports and Entertainment

Football is big news again, but I'll hold that for a while.

Theater news is sparse in the issues I have. On January 5, they've discontinued midweek shows. Basketball is in the news on January 12. On February 2, Girard looks like taking the boys' county championship, though the girls still have a chance for Jayton. The Kent County Interscholastic League meet is under way on Thursday, March 23, to continue on Friday and Saturday. The March 30 paper reports that Girard won the overall championship.

A new sport shows up. Amateur boxing had its opening night down at the Kent Theater on Friday, March 10. Another round of matches was held on March 17, and apparently another on March 24. Jiggs Holley lost the third fight.

And then I learn something new. Some of the Wade sons had apparently been writing some of the articles that I thought Mr. Wade wrote: "The fourth match was between two over-grown kids, Jack Powell of Spur, a kid in age, and Heb Wade (the writer of this article) a kid in mind. The bout was full of action in two rounds but the second round was slowed down somewhat by Wade who spent most of the round picking himself off the mat. The fight finally ended (after thirteen hours and forty-five minutes and three seconds) with both boys gasping for breath. The decision was in favor of both. A draw."

Softball shows up in the June 22 paper, with notice of plans to form a four-team league in Jayton. By the time the next week's paper appears, the first games have already been played. Reports on the city league games continue into August.

"Zorro Rides Again," the serial, apparently played down at the theater in December, January, and February. Sometime along in there, I got in trouble with Miss Kinney for distributing pictures of Zorro that I had drawn. Probably wasn't real trouble.

The Market Report

According to the January 19 paper, you could get forty-eight pounds of flour down at Robinson's for $1.35, a no. 2 can of peaches for 15 cents, a no. 2 can of grapefruit juice for a nickel, and two quarts of mustard for a quarter. At Bryant-Link, men's and boys' sweaters were available for 85 cents, and towels ranged from 5 cents to 25 cents.

On July 7, you could get a pound of wet wash done at the Jayton Laundry for 3 cents. At the grocery story, flour was $1.30 for forty-eight pounds, meal was 39 cents for twenty pounds, ten pounds of pintos was 60 cents, and a four-pound pail of coffee was 80 cents. At the dry goods store, ladies' hats cost $1.59, and panties, all sizes, were a quarter.

Prices don't seem to change too much during the rest of the year.

West Texas Utilities is still in business. On January 12, the *Chronicle* carries a long story out of Abilene that recounts some of the storm damage WTU dealt with during the preceding year. The story includes accounts of tornado damage at Clyde, the most severe of all, at Mertzon and San Angelo, lightning damage in Quanah, damage done by a runaway truck near Vernon, and flood damage in the Hill Country.

WTU workers also righted an Air Corps plane that flipped on landing at Abilene.

On March 2, "the approach of kite-flying days" prompts Mr. Bradley to caution boys against flying their kites near lines. In a story in the March 16 issue, Mr. Bradley invites the public down for the premier showing of the 1939 model Frigidaire. The WTU advertisement in the April 13 issue reminds folks of the free services available—FHA information, advice on lighting and kitchen planning, and information on planning for electric refrigeration, air conditioning, and electric cookery. The June 29 advertisement lists some of WTU's contributions to civic welfare: $489,983 in 1938 taxes, $1,200,000 payroll, and $150,000 in annual savings through rate reduction. It's not difficult to understand that they're talking about the state, not Jayton, or even Kent County.

School News and Late-Breaking Personals

The January 12 paper reports that the third grade (my grade, though not mine) is starting a unit on *Robinson Crusoe*. "We have turned our sand table into the island that Robinson Crusoe inhabited for so long. We will plant corn, maize, cotton and potatoes during the week and have reports every so often on our crops in the class." The honor roll report for the third grade on March 16 includes James Cox, Bobbie Nell Fuller, Bobby Elbert Hamilton, Lucille Robinson, Peggy Sue Robinson, Don Jones, Jimmy Matthews, and me. The April 27 report adds Maude Adele Brown, Olive Engledow, and Billy Glenn Vencil.

On May 11, the *Chronicle* reports that the seniors have taken a trip to Carlsbad Caverns, El Paso, and Juarez. A front-page notice in the August 24 paper announces that school will start on September 11 and lists the faculty. Miss Kinney is back for a second year in the third grade, but the story says that Miss Scarborough will be the fourth-grade teacher. She wasn't. Mrs. Check Jay was our teacher. I wonder what happened. On September 14, the *Chronicle* reports that, sure enough, school has opened, and with a large enrollment—might reach 275, the paper says. The October 26 paper has a big story about the PTA Halloween Carnival to be held up at the school on October 31. Apparently the fourth grade put on a play called *Jitney Jamboree*, in which, so the *Chronicle* says, I played a fat man. I have no recollection of the play. I do remember the carnival, but that was about all for us in Jayton. After that, soon after, I guess, we were gone.

29

So Far, 1939 Is Over, and We Are Gone

As I measure my recollections against the *Chronicle*'s rendition of sand-storms, I believe I have remembered them pretty well, though in my mind I've probably made them occur more frequently than they did. I doubt I deserve congratulations for remembering sandstorms – I've been in sandstorms since, and any blowing sandstorm down out of the north-west is a sure reminder of the others.

Other things I have not remembered so well, or have not remem-bered at all. Some things that I should remember, I cannot, because apparently I did not give them witness in the first place.

I have looked earnestly for my own name among the issues of the *Jayton Chronicle*, have wanted to see it as evidence that I was there.

I have found it, and ought to be reassured. I'm not.

Where was I those other times? I can't remember some things the *Chronicle* said I did, and have no recollection at all of much that I should have known and remembered well – water pumping through the fire hose from Credit Lake, Trades Day, later First Saturday, rodeos, softball games, barrel races, more softball games, the Green Castle Cafe, the name of the theater, and on, and on.

Maybe I wasn't there after all.

If I wasn't there at times and places when and where by any kind of reckoning I *should* have been, how can I be sure I was there at times and places when and where I *might* have been?

Since, I have looked for reminders of what I thought I saw, for the remainder of things I saw part of, have looked for authentication of what I thought I saw.

Example. In my mind, or wherever you keep such things, there are images, some clear, some cloudy, of marvelous airplanes that flew back when I was twelve to fifteen and older brothers were fighting World War II. The planes had striking names—Hurricane, Defiant, Avenger, Mustang, Corsair, Mosquito, Beaufighter, Thunderbolt, and on. I still sketch a fair Spitfire when I'm in committee meetings, and a passable Curtis P-40. But until I checked out Peter Bowers's *Forgotten Fighters and Experimental Aircraft*, I had quite forgotten one plane that I thought was especially thrilling to look at when I saw the pictures so long ago. There it was, on page 92, the Grumman XP-50, a two-engine fighter that never made it into production.

But it didn't disappear forever. Following a friend's advice (and I begin to think that his mind is as filled as mine is with rags and cactus and cotton bolls), I found it again. Les Daniels's book *Comix, A History of Comic Books in America*, has a six-page sample spread from the old comic book *Blackhawk*, which began publication under that name in 1944, and sure enough, in the last panel, having triumphed again over enemies of the Allies, the seven fierce heroes fly off in their Grumman XP-50s.

Once in a while, I go to the main library downtown for what some would call "real" reading, but mostly I follow the uncertain trail of a wonderfully trivial mind and take great pleasure in delightfully trivial joys. When I occasionally feel a need to justify myself, I think of it all as isometric exercises for the brain.

I fell into the habit of going to the public library when my children were young. When I'm working or studying, I go to the TCU Library. I haven't used it up. Most of it I haven't touched, or scarcely. It supports my work well enough, but it doesn't always feed my fancy, doesn't always yield what I want when I want to read and to look for fun. I've just about used up the TCU holdings in contemporary poetry. At first, then, in the earlier years, I depended on the downtown public library for more new poetry. There are 106 shelves of American poetry there, or about 370 feet, and I've still a way to go.

But then, especially in the last two or three years, I began to branch out. First it was to books about Texas. I didn't want regular old history books; I wanted oddities, backroads, county stories, especially from that stretch of Texas east of I-35 and north of I-20, and in the forty shelves (or some 140 feet) that I particularly haunt (the 976.4 series, and over in 917, too), have found books on Texas forts and Texas trails that I love, including Ray Miller's series, the *Eyes of Texas Travel Guide*.

Then it was over to the fine arts section, where there are some 750 shelves (about 2,600 feet) holding diverse visual arts and crafts. I've only just begun there. I've just about looked the pictures off the pages in Edwin Wade's *The Arts of the North American Indian* and Patricia Broder's *The American West, the Modern Vision*, and Michael Frary's *Impressions of the Texas Panhandle*. I've admired Gail Levin's book, *Hopper's Places*—it's a study of Edward Hopper's paintings against photographs of the places he painted, and the lessons in composition would benefit my freshman writing students. I've found books on wine label designs and book markers and California orange box labels and books on comic strips that let me catch up on Tarzan and Dick Tracy and Pogo and Peanuts and Wonder Woman. Reitburger and Fuchs's *Comics, Anatomy of a Mass Medium*, reminded me of The Phantom, a hero I never saw enough of when I was young. Maurice Horn's *Comics of the American West* showed me Rick O'Shay and Hipshot Percussion again.

On down in the fine arts section there are about a hundred shelves (about 350 feet) of books on the movies, and if I was not trivial before, I am now. I've found John Stanley's *Creature Features Movie Guide* and Jenni Calder's *There Must Be a Lone Ranger*, and books on horror and science fiction movies. In Alan Barbour's *A Thousand and One Delights* (mostly about escapist films of the forties), I found Claude Rains in "The

THERE IS
ONLY **ONE** PHANTOM!
THE **LORD** OF A
MIGHTY DOMAIN,
HE IS **THE GHOST**
WHO WALKS!
THERE IS **NONE**
OTHER!

Phantom of the Opera" and Lugosi's "Dracula," and Linda Stirling of "The Tiger Woman" in 1944, and eleven pages of photographs of Maria Montez in various roles. I see now that she ain't all that much to look at, but when I saw her in "Gypsy Wildcat" in 1944 and I was fourteen, I thought she was really something.

Barbour's *The Thrill of It All* (on B westerns) showed me Tom Mix and Buck Jones and Ken Maynard again, and Hoot Gibson and the Three Mesquiteers and Hopalong Cassidy. All this time, I remembered that his shirt and pants were solid black, but a still close-up shows that the pants are a dark stripe. Memory is usually wrong one way or another, one place or another. Barbour's *Days of Thrills and Adventures* (on serials) was best of all in this section. I found Buster Crabbe in "Flash Gordon," and right there on page 38, a still photo showing Zorro's first entrance in "Zorro Rides Again." God, he's wonderful. I was doing a pretty good business drawing pictures of Zorro for my third-grade friends when the teacher, Miss Kinney, caught me. It was a tragic moment for me, for I loved her deeply if not too wildly from afar.

And then there are airplane books, thirty-three shelves in three different locations, or some 115 feet. Wonderful pictures and wonderful

details: the nutty marvels in Bowers's *Unconventional Aircraft*, the trim little Curtis Goshawk in Taylor's *Warplanes of the World, 1918–1939,* the lovely little Boeing P-12 in Munson's *Warplanes of Yesteryear,* the wonderful little Gloster Gladiator in Green and Swanborough's *RAF Fighters.* On page 60 in Gunston's *An Illustrated Guide to Allied Fighters in World War II* was the best of all, that other beautiful airplane I had completely forgotten, the Westland Whirlwind, with its daring high tail, its slender fuselage, its two huge underslung engines. It doesn't get any better.

Lately, I've checked out Yann Lovelock's *The Vegetable Book,* and re-checked it. A splendid book, it tells the history of vegetables and how and where they struggled to cease being weeds and to become what

we eat. I don't know where the search will go from here, but I do know that it probably won't end. The ritual of the search, the ritual of being there, in the downtown public library with the recollection of books and my children, is too pleasurable for me to refrain. I go there maybe forty-five or forty-six Saturdays out of the fifty-two that a year gives. I find my treasures and check out, usually on the lower level that gives directly onto the stores and shops of the Tandy Center. I go up through Dillard's, check the fashions that I can't or won't achieve, and ease on over a block to Billy Miner's Saloon. Linda, who's pretty and pleasant and busy, brings me the drink that I've ordered maybe seventy-two times in a row. I think she has decided that it's what I want. Then, books in my bag on the stool beside me, I commence to hunt for the perfect peanut among the baskets they keep on the bar at Billy Miner's.

30

Missing Issues

I have no copies of the *Chronicle* for 1940. I wonder how things were, and what the news was, and what I might have learned from the missing issues.

I have no copies of the *Chronicle* for 1941. I still wonder how things were, and what the news was, and what I might have learned from the missing issues.

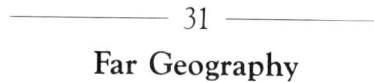

Far Geography

Sometimes, when I hear a child's call, say far down the block past the arching green trees, or maybe way over on the next street and down, or maybe just at twilight, I want to go and be her guard, or his, and teach the child safely home. Sometimes a child calls, far off, maybe just at twilight. Sometimes, I think I know who the child is and maybe where home is, and want to hold her safe, or him. Mostly, though, I doubt I can reach that far geography.

My family moved to Fort Worth in late 1939 when my father found a job at Purina Mill, and by the summer of 1941, our small exodus had taken us through many dwelling places. As I piece it out in my memory, we followed a downward slope in our domestic arrangements—the Purina job was not steady at first—through 801 Sylvania, an attic apartment, to 2800 East Fourth Street, half of a small house, to 914 Grace, half of another small house, to 3015 Bird, little more, I think, than a shanty behind someone's house, to 2500 Lillian, half of another small house. I didn't know much about it then and know less now, but I think my family was near bottom there when Purina at last put my father to work so regularly that he was to stay more than thirty years. After that, as I make things out now, there was a slow upward slope for us, through half of a house at 2424 Embry Place, and then, by 1941, to all of a small house at 809 Cleckler Street. We were to stay in that house and another on Cleckler Street for some years.

And by the fall of 1941, I had started in junior high school and discovered maps. I came to love them then, and have since. Perhaps I became obsessed with maps. I don't have a map *collection*. I don't search for rare old maps. But I am a fanatic looker and keeper.

The wall of my study upstairs is covered with maps, mostly the big fold-out maps that come periodically in the *National Geographic*. Over my desk is a big map of the United States. On either side are maps of England and Europe and Mexico and the West Indies and the Near East, and another map of the United States without state boundaries. It shows where American Indian tribes mostly lived once. Among

the maps, there is also a big poster, the one my daughter brought me that time, showing RAF planes. Behind me, on the other wall, are maps of the New England states and the southeastern states and the southwestern states and California and Africa.

I also have maps stacked and folded here, there, and yonder in my office in Reed Hall. The atlas of the United States—the one I look at most often—lies on top of books in a shelf close by my desk. It's worn. The cover is still there, but is no longer fastened to the book. On another shelf is a group of maps my daughter gave me once for Christmas —Caney Creek Wilderness and Ouachita National Forest in Arkansas, the Pecos Wilderness in the Carson and Santa Fe National Forests in New Mexico, the Caddo-Lyndon B. Johnson Grasslands, the whole Santa Fe National Forest, and the Davy Crockett National Forest.

Nearby is a pile of maps I accumulated once from the American Automobile Association for a trip to Washington, D.C. They took us across a long way, through Louisiana to Vicksburg and across Mississippi, then angling up through Alabama to Chattanooga and on by back roads to Gatlinburg and down onto the Blue Ridge Parkway and up through North Carolina and Virginia to Washington, then back down West Virginia and across Kentucky and down to Memphis and back across Arkansas and home.

Underneath that group of maps is a large envelope that holds more—maps that took us to the Big Bend, on up to El Paso, then up the west side of New Mexico and on to Durango, Colorado, and Mesa Verde, and back by Santa Fe and home. With them, rolled up and held by a rubber band, are four large county maps. They show King, Dickens, Kent, and Stonewall counties, all in sufficient detail to mark all farm and ranch houses and all roads, even the two-rut dirt roads that I've enjoyed. Farther down the shelf is a big heavy book that has enlarged maps of all 254 Texas counties. Beside it is a cardboard box with brown and orange stripes; it is filled with maps and notes from diverse places.

On my desk there is a new collection of maps from last summer. They tell how I drove alone across Arkansas and part of Tennessee and north across Kentucky and slantwise across Ohio and to Penn State University for a conference, and how I went on from there to Boston, where I met her plane, and we stayed in Cambridge, then went to Concord, Vermont, and from there drove to Portsmouth and to the White Mountains and across the Kancamagus Highway and to Freeport, Maine, and then on southward, down across Massachusetts and Connecticut and through New York City and down the New Jersey turnpike and alongside Philadelphia and across corners of Delaware and Maryland and by Baltimore and Washington and down through Virginia and North Carolina to Myrtle Beach, and then at last home across South Carolina and Georgia and Alabama and Mississippi and Louisiana.

I came to love maps in the seventh grade, and have ever since. I know that maps aren't territories, and I am sometimes lost.

If I became obsessed with maps in the seventh grade, I didn't know I was obsessed. I doubt I knew the word. I just looked. Perhaps I had not seen many maps before that time. I can't remember. But that year I was in a geography class, and the textbook was big and filled with maps. In those days, we had a required study hall during one period. I didn't much like doing my homework in study hall, so spent the entire period, day after day, week after week, looking at the wonderful maps in my geography book. I wanted to know the names of places—and more, to keep the names. I made lists, lists of countries and rivers and mountains and deserts, lists of cities and towns and villages. I still don't know why.

Perhaps I just wanted to know the names of things.

Perhaps I was feeling a little lost in the big city. We had come to a place where 200,000 and more people were all together with houses on houses, buildings on buildings, from a little town of 700 souls. (I've told my children that this figure doesn't include Boone Bilberry, that you couldn't count him: the Baptists said he didn't have a soul, and

besides, he was often a little fuzzy around the edges and sometimes disappeared altogether. Mr. Bilberry drank a little. I made him up.) I had been used to empty places, and now, wherever I walked, I couldn't find any. I had been used to the places I knew, and now, wherever I walked, I couldn't find them.

Some things haven't changed all that much. I am still lost from that other country and can't find myself there, or sometimes here. I have no scrapbooks of the lost country except for the fragments in my mind and—now—some issues of the *Chronicle*, though I do cherish a few photographs I made around Jayton and Spur and in the Croton Breaks. While I have never learned to believe in photographs, I have fingered two in particular so much that they are bent and wrinkled.

One shows the little house where we lived on the Lowrance place, right on the rim between the edge of Jayton and the first canyon in the Breaks. When I made the picture years later, it was being used for hay storage. Sometime later, they took it down, or maybe it fell down. I look at the picture, but I can't find the house, or myself in it. The other picture was taken from the highway a few miles southeast of Spur, looking up under the railroad trestle to the rise and my grandfather's farmhouse. Trestle and house are gone now, and when I look at the picture, I can't find all of us there or see just what the place was like in those times. For that matter, I can't find Jayton, even when I'm looking at it.

Once in a while, it works out, and I can find things, get my directions straight. Mostly not, even when I ponder maps, as I still do. The maps in my office make for wonderful looking, thought I don't make lists any more. The atlas is well-thumbed. I take it with me on most trips, and sometimes look at the map almost as much as I look at the territory. I know that the map isn't the territory, and I'm sometimes lost, can't always find places. Maps don't always do me much good. Sometimes a fellow can look and look and still not find places. Finding places is hard if you lose your direction, and I've often done so, though not always.

When I was young, I was drafted into the army and spent about eighteen months in Germany. I was stationed at Coleman Barracks just outside Mannheim, where the Neckar flows into the Rhine, about ten miles from Heidelberg. I saw a lot of southern Germany, both on duty and off, but I never knew which way was north. I wasn't, as they say, "turned around"; I couldn't make any guess at all about direction, even when the sun came up where it was supposed to. I got about well enough by doing what I was told to do and by riding trains and buses whose drivers seemed to know where they were going.

But I've also been in Chicago, and my sense of direction is pretty sure there, though I don't congratulate myself all that much: I'm probably sure of direction because Lake Michigan is there, and no matter how I might confuse things, Lake Michigan is probably going to be east of the city.

I never know how it's going to work out. One spring I went to a conference in Atlanta, and not only didn't know which way was north (it was dark and cloudy), but scarcely knew which way was up.

However, at another conference in San Diego, I kept things pretty straight. It's pretty hard to misplace the Pacific Ocean.

But in Philadelphia, I never did get situated right with the sun and so was never sure about direction.

I know how to get around in Washington, though. The Mall runs east and west and the White House is north of the Mall and just northwest of the Mall is the building where my daughter worked that time and just south of the Mall, on the Tidal Basin, is the Jefferson Memorial.

And I know how to get around in West Texas, even if the places I get to aren't always what I thought they were.

And I keep looking at maps, looking to know where places are, hunting to know their names, wanting to know how they came there and why and what the names signify. One summer I drove from the campus of Penn State University, in the middle of the state, westward to Pittsburgh. Along the way, I came upon a road sign that said it was four miles to Nanty Glo. That seemed a strange name. When I got back home and to the library, I found a travel guide that explained it. The name is Welsh and means "coal stream," or "the stream where coal was found," and was apparently given by Welsh miners who settled there.

I don't know why Muleshoe was named Muleshoe or why Cut and Shoot was so named, but I do know that Spur was named after the Spur Ranch and that Jayton was named for the founding Jay family. Mrs. Check Jay, a daughter-in-law of that family whose real first name was Cherokee, was my fourth-grade teacher, but I was then still in love with Miss Kinney, my third-grade teacher, and had not yet found my way fully into Mrs. Jay's grade.

Finding your way is hard if you can't get directions straight.

Some people seem to preserve their sense of direction in every aspect of their lives. Not long ago, I visited one afternoon with a young colleague. He knows where he is going. His direction is clear to him. He has a "game plan" for his life—he put it that way. He has "prioritized" his tasks and his goals. He put it that way. I hope a bolt of lightning comes and searches me out if I ever use the word *prioritize*, except as it comes from the mouth of someone else. He knew which way was north and up.

I know a university administrator who always gets his directions straight. He won't entertain an idea, however good or provocative it may be, unless the proposer of the idea also provides the plan for "operationalizing" the idea. I don't much want to say that word either, but he knows which way is north.

I prefer west. I sing a little tune with these words (if you'll imagine you hear a guitar telling the rhythm):

> The lines of the map separate my parts.
> The edge of the open runs up my chest.
> Wherever I stand is the Great Divide,
> And I check the weather looking west.
>
> The cities of the north are always *up*,
> And the cities of the south are *down*.
> Wherever I stand is the Great Divide—
> I always say *over* for an eastern town.

Up in Tulsa, over in Durham,
Down in Houston and New Orleans.
Wherever I stand is the Great Divide,
And it's *out* in Abilene.

Up in Scranton, down in Beaumont,
Over in Macon and Tupelo.
Wherever I stand is the Great Divide,
And it's out in San Angelo.

The lines of the map separate my parts.
The edge of the open runs up my chest.
Wherever I stand is the Great Divide,
And I check the weather looking west.

Sometimes, I know which way is which. Sometimes, I stumble and grope, hoping, as the Mormons sang, "We'll find the place that God for us has blessed / Far away in the West."

The maps are dear to me. I know that they're maps, not places. When we make maps, or when we write, we're trying to render one kind of experience through another kind of experience, a territory through pictures, a life through words.

The pictures and the words, then, are going to be imperfect, but they will hold and last a while and we can send small messages out about how things looked, maybe get little replies. I've wanted, most of my life, to catch moments and days and events and places and hold them, mark them, keep them. I can't, but perhaps that's why I cherish maps. A map will hold a while as things change, places change, time passes, and we go on. They are treasures. They are imperfect, but treasures, even if I'm sometimes lost and cannot find those far geographies.

32

Nineteen Forty-two

When I come back to Jayton in the *Chronicle* after the long silence of 1940 and 1941, the world has changed, though some tunes remain from times before. The paper for February 12, 1942, carries this headline: "Jayton Reared Youth Meets Death in Airplane Accident," and this story, out of Phoenix, Arizona: "Four Army Air Corps cadets crashed to their deaths and a fifth parachuted to safety when a flight of training planes en route from Luke Field, Ariz. to El Paso, Texas, encountered a blinding rain storm near Hachits, N.M. Monday night." One of them was Charlie Coats, 24, most recently of Lubbock, but reared in Jayton. He was the first local boy to die in the war. The next issue of the paper, for February 19, reports on his funeral in Jayton.

THE WAR

The first issue of the year, on January 1, reports that a National Defense school will begin on Monday, January 5, up at the school, with classes in metal work, blacksmithing, and electric welding, "with special emphasis on repair and care of farm machinery." The same issue reports that the army will now accept enlistments by married men without dependents. The January 15 issue shows a letter on the front page addressed to the Honorable L. F. Wade, Chairman, Kent County Defense Committee: "It is not necessary for me to call your attention to the urgency of this matter. All Americans fully realize the gravity of the situation at the present time. It is absolutely necessary that your County Committee start functioning immediately so as to be sure that you exceed this minimum allotment during the year. Your minimum allotment for Kent County is $89,000."

The right-hand column of the front page in this issue is "A Week of the War," the first of many such columns summarizing war news. Inside appears the first listing of Red Cross War Fund contributions. Contributions this time range from six cents to twenty dollars. Herschel Durham is down for a dollar. That's my uncle Herschel, Aunt Edith's husband. War news on February 26 included this: "Yes, a Jap sub shelled a spot on the Pacific Coast this week. They killed two back-up bugs, two sand crabs and a lizard. The Japs are great fighters (cowardly killers) when your back is turned toward them." The March 19 paper announces that General Douglas MacArthur has arrived in Australia to take command of all armed forces in the East Indies.

The April 9 issue carries this notice, "Kent County Called Upon to Buy $30,000 Worth of Victory War Bonds," with an appeal by L. F. Wade, Chairman, War Bond Sales Committee, Kent County. This issue also says that the Fisher Body Works of Detroit has just built its first all-welded 30-ton tank from start to finish in just forty-nine days, and that a company in Portland, Oregon, is building one ten-thousand-ton Liberty freighter every five days. The June 4 paper says profit from the upcoming Texas Cowboy Reunion in Stamford will go to buy war bonds. The June 11 paper announces that Kent County made good on its May quota for war bonds, buying $1,937.50 against an allotment of $1,100.

I learn from the August 27 issue about the "saga of General Mikhailo-vich" and his Yugoslav army. The September 3 paper says that "with American farmers being called on to produce more and more with less and less, the need for cooperation and sharing the use of certain kinds of machinery is due to result in the organization of many farmer coop-eratives in Kent County." The same issue announces a September quota of $4,500 in bonds. A note in the October 29 issue says, "Hell's a pop-pin' in the Solomons and Uncle Sam is again paying dearly for her un-preparedness, thanks to the isolationists."

In the November 5 issue, I learn a little about the "lost battalion," — the Second Battalion, 131st Field Artillery — made up largely of young men from West Texas. They were already in Java when the war broke out. The commandant of Dutch cadets training in Midland reports that there has been no Japanese claim of capture, that the troops are estab-lished in the mountains, harassing the Japanese. No official report on the unit has been received since February. The Dutch officer reports that food should be plentiful — sweet potatoes, rice, breadfruit, bananas, cucumbers, melons, other wild fruit, wild chickens, wild pigs, and other wild game. H. J. Whatley of Jayton is a member of this unit.

And the war comes to Jayton in other ways. The March 12 paper announces that war rationing books have been received by the county clerk. The April 23 issue notifies everyone that the registration period for rationing books is May 4–7. Scrap drives are announced on Janu-ary 22, and that comes home to Kent County in the February 5 paper: "Kent County Farmers Urged To Sell Their Scrap Iron," with the sub-head, "Old Cultivator Seat May Get a Jap." "There are five hundred farms in Kent County," the story says. "Almost every farm has at least one hundred pounds of old scrap iron lying around the place which is of no value to the farmer." The February 26 paper reports on the cen-sus of automobile graveyards that has been undertaken, and reckons that warships can be made from abandoned jalopies. By August 13, an "all-out scrap metal drive" is coming to an end, and Kent County has a quota of one hundred tons. Scrap Day in Jayton is August 29.

Meanwhile, life goes on, or doesn't. The February 12 paper says that the rural electrification program has been delayed until after the war. The July 30 paper reports "How They Voted in Kent County": W. Lee O'Daniel still gets most votes for governor. Uncle Herschel didn't win his race for county commissioner. On September 17, I learn that new car license plates will be miniatures — one-inch by four-inch strips to be bolted onto old licenses. The October 29 issue says that Gulf Oil is exploring in the Clairemont area for possible oil drilling sites. The November 5 issue announces that November 13–14 is the time to register for gas rationing cards. The same paper says the election "went off very quiet in Kent County. No riots, no fights, no drunks, no arrests, all Democrats elected.–Believe It or Not."

But the war came to Jayton and Kent County more noticeably, more immediately than I have reported. The first notice I see in my microfilm papers is in the January 22 issue, announcing the third draft registration, for February 16. It is to include "all unregistered males who were born between February 17, 1897, and December 31, 1921." The same paper reports that Sergeant Q. T. Wade, son of Mrs. Astena Wade of Clairemont, is probably a prisoner of the Japanese. Sergeant Wade had been in the marines for some years and was on Wake Island when it was attacked. The February 5 and February 12 issues again remind everyone of the February 16 registration.

The April 9 paper has the first of many notices I see under the heading "Leave for Service"–though I've obviously missed some in absent papers: "Five more Kent County boys left this week to take up their duties with Uncle Sam's fighting forces." I don't recognize any of the names. I wish I did. The April 9 issue also says that the armed forces have grown fast: "At the present time there are slightly more than 2,000,000 men in the American Army. There are 1,000,000 more in the Navy, and about 500,000 in the Air Force. That marks an immense change from a few years ago when the Army was down to around 150,000 and the other military branches were also negligible so far as numbers are concerned."

But it's not enough, the story says; the total will probably have to grow to twelve million. The April 23 paper announces the fourth draft registration for April 27. On May 5, I learn that State Senator Marshall Formby from Dickens County has been sworn in as a private, and the May 21 issue reports that "again Texas is in the spotlight. According to the news dispatches from Washington, there were more Texans in the air raid on Japan than men from any other state in the union." The young men of Texas, the story goes on, "are not appeasers and neither are they isolationists. They are not out to pick a fight but if any fighting has to be done you will find them on the job passing out rights and lefts, rights and lefts, until the enemy is either dead or crying calf rope until one can hear him around the world." The same paper says that Sergeant Q. T. Wade is indeed a prisoner of the Japanese in a camp somewhere near Shanghai.

By May 28, the roll of Kent County soldiers, sailors, and marines includes ninety-four young men, plus one added in a correction the next week. The June 11 paper gives an account of the "lost battalion" that the Dutch commandant would later be more hopeful about:

H. J. Whatley Missing in Action

One of the mysteries that may not be solved until the war's close is the fate of the Second Battalion of the 131st Field Artillery, composed almost entirely of West Texas Guardsmen and last heard of in Java. The War Department has reported belatedly that these 600 men presumably are prisoners of the Japanese. Some of them probably have been killed in action, however, and there has been an unconfirmed report that some escaped to the hills to engage in guerilla fighting.

. . . H. J. Whatley, son of Jeff Whatley of Jayton, is one of the members of this battalion, and his many friends in Jayton are hoping and trusting that he is still alive and well, where ever he may be.

The same paper reports that Donald H. Cox, grandson of Mrs. J. H. Donoho, is a prisoner: "He was one of the New Mexico National Guard troops that landed on Bataan just before the Japs struck and was taken prisoner when Bataan was captured." The June 18 issue announces the fifth draft registration date, and also says that seven more "Kent County boys" have gone off to war. According to the July 2 paper, Jack Hunnicutt of Girard has been promoted to sergeant, and the July 23 issue gives notice that twelve more young men have gone off to the service.

In the August 20 issue, Jesse Holley writes to Mr. Wade to thank him for sending the *Chronicle*, and the paper reports that thirteen more have gone off to the services. Byron Smith writes in the September 3 paper that he hasn't been getting the *Chronicle*, but has "plenty of eats and all the care a soldier should have" where he is at Camp Carson, Colorado. The September 10 paper says a recruiting officer will be at the post office on September 15, and on September 17, I learn that a bill to draft eighteen-year-olds had been introduced in Washington. Jesse Holley, the paper says on September 24, has written to his folks in Jayton to say that he has been shipped out, but can't say where.

Nine more young men have gone, according to the October 1 paper, and the October 8 issue says four have enlisted in the Air Corps. The October 22 *Chronicle* says that "the West Texas Army Recruiting District led in September enlistments in the Eighth Service Command." The same paper has this: "Halley Wade of the Navy, who is attending torpedo school in San Diego, writes that he has passed his examination for rating as a Seaman 1st Class, is feeling fine and enjoying his school."

That's one of Mr. Wade's sons. The October 29 paper reports that nine more young men have gone, and the November 26 issue tells that six more have left.

CROPS AND GOODS

The January 1 paper says that the state cotton allotment is slightly smaller than it was for 1941, and the January 22 issue reports that crop loans are now available through the Farm Credit Administration. Kent County gins, I learn on February 5, have handled 11,591 bales of cotton, way up from the report in January of 1941. Sugar rationing plans will go into effect soon, the February 12 *Chronicle* says, and the February 19 paper says that now is the time to build terraces. In the February 26 issue, B. F. Vance, chairman of the Texas USDA War Board, announced "Plant for Victory" week and said that he hoped no farmer would enter planting season "without full personal knowledge of his wartime food production responsibilities." The March 26 issue reports that 11,784 bales have come in from the 1941 crop, and the May 14 paper says that what had in drought times been a burdensome surplus of cotton is now a "valuable stockpile."

I learn that grasshopper poison is now available from the June 4 *Chronicle*, that those aiming to can fruit in the fall had better start planning ahead how to do it with sugar rationed, and that a "Victory Cake" can be made without sugar: ½ cup shortening, 2 teaspoons orange rind, 1 cup corn syrup, 2½ cups flour, ½–¼ teaspoon salt, 2 eggs, ½ cup milk, 1½ teaspoons vanilla, 2 teaspoons baking powder. The July 16 *Chronicle* reports a considerable infestation of boll weevils in Kent County cotton.

A cautionary note on August 6 says, "Jayton folks are urgently requested to conserve their water. The City is down to one pump now and it's impossible to say when we will be able to get another. Use water when you have to. Not when you want to." The next week's paper says "the water problem in Jayton is and always has been a problem and it shows little improvement, in fact it gets more serious as the days and months go by." The story reports a raise in the water rate for Jayton.

Loans at 85 percent parity are available on this year's cotton crop, the August 20 paper says, and the August 27 paper thinks that two and a half inches of August rain help make crop prospects brighter. The first bale of cotton came in on Wednesday, August 26; it weighed 428 pounds and sold for eighteen cents a pound. Under the heading "Harvest Time," the September 17 *Chronicle* observes: "Yes, there is a way to tell when fall time and harvest time arrives that's when traveling shows begin to put in their appearance. All next week an old-time medicine show is billed for Jayton, and the sick and the near sick and those who think they are sick or hope to be sick will have an opportunity to lay in a supply of the one medicine on earth that will cure every known ailment of mankind." The paper for October 15 urges more people to raise stock for meat at home and announces loans from the Farm Security Administration for farm women who need assistance in food preservation and storage. The loans can go toward purchase of pressure cookers, jars, and other necessities. And the November 26 paper announces coffee rationing.

The Weather

The *Chronicle* doesn't afford me much weather news this year. The April 9 paper says, "Continued Rain Puts Extra Fine Season in Ground." The June 25 issue reports a freakish storm on June 20, with high winds and uncommonly hot temperatures, as if "the world was on fire. . . . Crops suffered greatly, more especially young tender cotton and gardens. The sand rolled and the air was filled with dust that left its mark on everything." On September 24, the paper reports that fall is here, that it arrived on Friday, September 18, at exactly 12 o'clock midnight: "The temperature dropped about thirty degrees sudden like and in making the dive knocked the bung hole out of the rain barrel and by noon Saturday two and one half inches of water had run out, making this about the wettest, muddiest, sloppiest, country we have ever lived in for several months."

Seems like mostly they just had weather in 1942.

The News — Local and Personal

The January 15 paper says that Mr. and Mrs. Martin Meador and son have moved to Arkansas. That's my Aunt Mary and family, and I don't guess I knew they had lived in Arkansas. Uncle Martin is dead now, Aunt Mary lives in Pecos, and their son, Royce, is I guess still in New Mexico. Aunt Mary sent me later to see Joy Kidd, who sent me to Jerry Parker, to whom I finally returned the *Chronicle* microfilms. The same paper tells about a John Jones of Brandon, Mississippi, visiting kin in Jayton this week, and I wonder if that's Don Jones's father, and have they gone from Jayton, too? The Jayton Culture Club met at Mrs. Fowler's home, with twelve members and two guests.

The "Personals" now are often items about servicemen visiting home. The April 9 issue carries a display urging "variety meats" for "war menu planning—liver, kidney, heart, tongue, tripe, sweetbreads, and brains." The April 23 issue says that Tom Wade of Lamesa visited his parents, Mr. and Mrs. L. F. Wade, last weekend. Tom was my brother's other best friend, along with Red Robinson. Had he graduated from high school and taken a job in Lamesa? But then the May 28 issue says maybe otherwise. I've already mentioned Halley Wade a little earlier. A notice appears in this issue telling about Halley's departure for the navy. Halley had been "a mainstay" in the *Chronicle* office, Mr. Wade reports, while sister Alice had had charge of local news gathering and advertising. Older brothers are already gone, Herbert to a bomber squadron in Puerto Rico, Robert in an officer's training course. And now Halley. Mr. Wade reports: "We are going to be somewhat handicapped in the office for a week or so, but we will make it, for when Halley stepped out, Tom, the last of the brood, stepped in and the old linotype keeps clacking and the presses will keep rolling and in time us Americans will whip the hell out of Hitler and his Jap allies and when the boys come marching home we will have a big family reunion and all start all over again, in a better and cleaner world."

It looks as if Peggy Sue Robinson is gone from Jayton, too. A note in the August 20 issue says that "Mr. and Mrs. Bake Robinson and Peggy of Post visited in Jayton Sunday. Peggy stayed for a few days' visit with relatives." The October 8 issue says they were back for another visit. The September 3 paper says that Bobbie Nell Fuller went with her parents to attend graduation exercises at Texas Tech. Verdie Mae Fuller graduated. I guess that must be Bobbie Nell's sister. Near the end of the year, on October 22, the *Chronicle* lambasts the "starvation allowances" given military dependents: "The allowances given dependents of America's fighting men amount to a national disgrace." Dependents of private soldiers received allowances ranging from fifteen to fifty dollars a month.

SPORTS AND ENTERTAINMENT

Football is still news, though I'll save that for later, and I have little sports news otherwise in my copies of the paper.

The theater is now the TEXAN, and apparently it had a bad summer. A story in the September 10 paper says the theater has only been open on weekends, but will be back showing full-time, three movies a week, starting September 11. Harley Sadler brought his traveling theatrical company to town in October.

The Market Report

The January 15 *Chronicle* says that at Gardner Brothers Grocery you can get a hundred pounds of pinto beans for $4.50, forty-eight pounds of flour for $1.49, a gallon of syrup for 54 cents, a good broom for 33 cents, a pound of ginger snaps for 10 cents, and a pound of coffee for 29 cents. At Bryant-Link, a pair of men's Justin boots came as low as $13.95.

By July 2, flour was up to $1.89 for forty-eight pounds, but coffee was down to 23 cents a pound. A dozen eggs would get you 30 cents in trade. At the dry goods store, men's shantung summer pants were $1.95, cotton slips were 79 cents, satin slips were 98 cents, and silk hose ranged from a dollar to a dollar and a quarter.

On November 26, pinto beans are a nickel a pound at Gardners, flour is up to $1.95, five pounds of jelly costs 75 cents, a quart of peanut butter is 40 cents, and a can of chili is a dime. The Texan Theater was about to show "The Gay Caballero" with Caesar Romero on Friday and Saturday, "Look Who's Laughing" with Edgar Bergen and Charlie Mc-Carthy at the Saturday night preview and on Sunday and Monday, and "Junior Army" with Freddy Bartholomew, on Tuesday, Wednesday, and Thursday.

WTU is there. In a front-page story on March 12, officials are urging everyone to take good care of electric appliances because the manufacturers have converted to production of war materials. In another front-page story on March 26, Mr. Bradley cautions youngsters about flying kites near wires. The WTU advertisement in the April 23 issue focuses on care for electric appliances, with specific tips on care of refrigerators, washers, water heaters, and ranges on small appliances. The July 30 advertisement quotes a letter:

> I learned about light in a blackout. We had our first practice blackout here recently. For twenty minutes, my family and I sat in total darkness. The seriousness of war hit us all harder than ever before.
> Then, when the all-clear sounded and we turned the lights back on, warmth and reassurance came into the room. That made me

realize that whatever I spend for electricity, it's still about the cheapest thing I buy.

The advertisement for November 5 has a picture of a line team in the wires, waving to a flight of bombers overhead. Below, there is a dialogue between Reddy Kilowatt and Adolf Hitler:

> *Adolf:* Dot humming—vit iss it?
>
> *Reddy:* That, Adolf, is the hum of power by which you will meet your doom. Power in the air . . . power afoot, on tap to build more planes, more tanks, more guns, more ships. It's the hum of American men and machines at work—twenty-four hours a day!

And so on.

SCHOOL NEWS

The February 12 *Chronicle* shows the school honor roll. In the seventh grade, where I might have been, Lucille Robinson, Jimmy Cox, Billy Vencil, and Margie Myrick are listed. The July 2 paper reports that, by the results of an election, several small schools will consolidate with Jayton. The Clipper, Luzon, Rosewood, and Henson communities joined Jayton in the election. The September 3 issue announces that school will begin on Monday, September 7. The September 10 paper reports the opening under a new superintendent, Mr. Stewart, and lists the teachers. Mrs. Fowler is still the first-grade teacher. Mrs. Check Jay has moved up to fifth grade. Looks like Bobbie Nell Fuller's sister, now called Verda Mae Fuller, is the new second- and third-grade teacher.

33

The Saga of the Jayton Jaybirds, 1938–46, as Told in the Incomplete Files of the *Jayton Chronicle* and Modified by Failed Memory and Faulty Interpretation

I remember them in the stunning light of fall afternoons in West Texas, the sun already slanting toward them from far in the west, the light sure and sharp and clear and golden, their shadows blue and deep and palpable against the light as bright as ever Greek light was, and more hurtful.

I remember them big and quick, bound for glory—Raymond Patton, the fullback, into the line again and again; Buzz Daniels, the halfback, sweeping end again and again (they didn't have all that many different plays); Jay Wade, the end, going up that time, twisting in the air, taking the pass down near the five-yard line right where I stood, turning, lunging across the goal so Jayton could beat Spur; little Jack Patton, the quarterback, governing it all; my brother, the left guard, going high that time to intercept the pass, taking it though they didn't want him to have it, running, running. I remember them in their splendid yellow jerseys, with black across the shoulders, black numbers on their chests and backs, clacking out of the dressing room, huge and strong and casual, helmets swinging in their hands, my brother, number nine, among them.

I remember them so, have sometimes remembered them well, have sometimes missed in memory altogether, have sometimes made my narrative from the misremembered truths and unobserved events that some call lies. They are not lies. They are sweet and strong in the stunning light that slants across them from the west.

I remember the field, down the slope west from the school. They played on the red earth, not on grass, when they played at home. I remember watching Mr. Coons draw the yard lines with a hoe. I remember watching them practise. I thought I watched them every day, but I probably didn't: memory often turns the occasional into the continuous. I don't even know whether or not I saw all of the games they played at home. I thought I did, but I don't know now.

I have told the story repeatedly, to my children, to friends, to passing strangers who lingered too long, how in 1938, Jayton decided to have a football team up at the high school for the very first time, how my brother, still a sophomore and weighing only 135 pounds (or 130, or 140, depending on when I tell the story), was the starting left guard for that very first team.

The *Chronicle* tells the story somewhat differently. I had much of the story wrong; some of it I never knew, and still don't. I don't have all the issues of the *Chronicle*, don't know that I have the text of Jayton Jaybird football, don't know that I would read it well if I did have it. I don't know, for example, why they were called "Jaybirds," or why the colors yellow and black were chosen. Were yellow and black uniforms the cheapest?

At any rate, the *Chronicle* tells the story somewhat differently. The *Chronicle* for September 15, 1938, begins like this:

JAYTON FOOTBALL TEAM ROUNDING INTO SHAPE

For the first time in many years Jayton will have a football team to yell for and from observation of practice it is going to be a good one to start yelling for.

Last Tuesday afternoon we went up and watched Coaches Williams and Williams put the boys through their paces and although the boys are light and inexperienced they are catching on to the game in a hurry. Most of these boys are fast and when they get hold of the ball they know how to move their feet. With a little more time to teach the fundamentals of the game we predict that

Jayton will have one of the best little teams in this part of the country.

A total of 22 boys were on the field in suits and listening and doing their best to carry out the advice of their coaches. Some getting fingers in their eyes and others getting hands and shins scratched but not a whimper do you hear. This is the kind of boys that will make a real football team and we are for them 100 per cent.

The first game on the incomplete schedule is set for September 23 against Rotan second string.

So, there it was on the first page. I'd been wrong all those years. This was not Jayton's first football team. I was wrong about other things, too.

Across the page, in a story announcing the opening of school on September 12, is a list of the boys who have reported for football practice: Jack Patton, Buzz Daniels, Floyd Hall, Darwin Sproules, Ross Inglish, Kenneth Davis, John H. Montgomery, Billy McLaury, Jiggs Holley, Raymond Patton, Jesse Ward Holley, Tom Bill Fowler, Bake Robinson (that's Peggy Sue's older brother), James Wallace Jay (that's P-Sam), Earl Tally, Sam Matthews, E. S. Gallagher, LeRoy Boland, J. W. Casey, Richard Robinson (that's Red Robinson, my brother's good friend and Peggy Sue's next older brother), Tom Wade (the editor's son and my brother's other best friend), Nolan Corder (that's my brother), and Travis Thompson.

The next week's paper, dated September 22, has for its major headline on page one, "Jayton 'II' First Game at Rotan Friday," and the story reminds all that the game will start at eight o'clock in Rotan: "The 1938 edition of the Jayton football team, the first in over ten years, will go on parade Friday nite at Rotan for the first game of the year. This will not only be the first game that the Jayton boys have played this year but the first game they ever played and some of the boys have never seen a football game." The reporter didn't get a starting line-up, but my brother's name is in the list of those who will see some action Friday night. I have no copies of the *Chronicle* for the next month. My recollection is that Rotan won by 40 to 6, but my recollection is often wrong.

The next notice is on Thursday, October 27, announcing a game the next day in Jayton against Fluvanna. I don't remember Fluvanna. A report of the previous game follows, but the score is missing:

> The local football team will encounter a new foe on Friday. They know very little about the tactics of Fluvanna but we have heard they will send a strong team to oppose the local Jay Birds.
> Last week Jayton played a team from Spur and had a good game.

Daniels scored on an end run during the early part of the game but a try for point went haywire.

Spur threatened to score in the last quarter. A good return punt by Patton and a fumble by Spur helped us out of the pinch.

Come out Friday to see the Jay Birds play Fluvanna.

In the following week's paper, dated November 3, I learn that Jayton prevailed:

Holding Fluvanna almost powerless for all but a few seconds of play at the same time clicking with their scoring machine the Jay Birds rang up their third victory of the season having beaten a team from Spur only a week before and defeating Peacock in a close fought contest during the County Fair.

The 14–0 shellacking of the team from Fluvanna gave the Jay Birds a .6 per cent rating and gave them hope of beating Swenson in the game Friday.

During the second quarter, after having played in their end of the field most of the evening, Buzz Daniels on an off tackle play crashed through for the first tally of the game. Patton converted for the extra point.

Again during the last quarter, after Fluvanna had threatened to score by a long run back of a punt and several ground gaining plays, Jayton took the ball and after a series of first downs made possible by the successful ball carrying of Hall, Patton, Daniels and a completed pass from the hands of little Jack Patton, helped along by a blocked punt by Gat Cox, Daniels again crashed over for the second touchdown after a nice end run of 20 yards. Patton again converted for the extra point.

This was truly the best game of the season. The linemen, Jay, Inglish, Matthews, Cox, Fowler, Davis, were outstanding. The backfield also took time and after a short while began finding the holes left by the linemen and took advantage of their improved playing.

Bake Robinson, charging back for the Jay Birds, was injured early in the first quarter and did not see much action.

Flash Holley and Fighting Fowler were active substitutes.

I notice right away that the account does not mention my brother, and I wonder why.

The next game is against Swenson on Friday, November 4. I don't know how that game came out. Jayton apparently won and apparently played again on Wednesday, November 9, for the *Chronicle* of November 10 reports not only the Swenson game, but also a 6–0 win over Colorado Springs on Wednesday, the end of a "successful football season," with four wins, one tie, and two losses.

But the next week's paper, for November 17, says that the Athletic

Association of Jayton High School has decided to add two or three more games. The first of these is scheduled for Thursday evening, November 17, against the Stamford B team. Perhaps you'll remember that in this part of the country, *evening* doesn't mean a night game.

That's all of Jayton Jaybird, or Jayton Jay Bird, football for 1938. I have no other account until September, 1939.

The *Chronicle* for September, 1939, reports that twenty players have begun training for a tough schedule. The story lists the players and their weights: Richard Robinson, 130; T. R. Hamilton, 135; D. C. Vandiver, 128; Jack Patton, 130; LeRoy Boland, 156; Kenneth Davis, 146; Bill Daniels, 153; E. S. Gallagher, 150; Buzz Daniels, 150; Rex (Gatlin) Cox, 149; Tom Bill Fowler, 135; Jesse Ward Holley, 144; Cotton Thompson, 150; Floyd Hall, 156; Tom Wade, 154; Sam Matthews, 147; Nolan Corder, 140; Clyde Goff, 135. That's eighteen, though the headline said twenty had reported.

The issue for September 14, 1939, reports that the schedule is not yet complete, but that the boys will play Spur, Leuders, Hamlin, Stamford, Swenson, Colorado, and Peacock, with two more games still to be scheduled.

I found a surprise in the September 28, 1939, issue. A front-page story reports that Jayton has defeated Spur, 19–13, in the season opener: "The starting line-up: Rex Cox, fullback; Buzz Daniels and Floyd Hall, halfbacks; Jack Patton, quarterback; Kenneth Davis and Bill Daniels, ends; LeRoy Boland and Tom Bill Fowler, tackles; Sam Matthews and Jesse Ward Holley, guards; and Hubert Knight, center; played the entire game with one substitution, Nolan Corder at guard for Holley who received a slight injury." There it was: he wasn't the starting guard, apparently never had been. The same issue reports that the football boys were given a big chicken barbeque dinner on Tuesday night, September 26, and that they're to play Leuders on Friday afternoon, September 29. I don't know how the Leuders game turned out.

The *Chronicle* for October 12, 1939, reports that on Friday, October 6, Hamlin won 48–0, in "the bloodiest slaughter ever seen by the Jayton Footballers." But then, inside the paper, there is a complete play-by-play account of the entire game. It begins with the starting line-ups, and *there is my brother at guard.*

The issue for October 19, 1939, announces that the team will take on the Stamford B team today. In the paper for the following week, dated October 26, I learn that Jayton won 26–0. The next game, the same story says, is scheduled for Friday, November 3, in Jayton, against

Swenson. I can't get the time exactly right, but I'd guess it was my brother's last game. We left for the big city some time around then. There is, at any rate, no further report on football for 1939: I have no issues of the *Chronicle* again until December 29. By that time, football and my family are long gone.

There's more Jayton Jaybird football, after the long silence of 1940 and 1941, but I had already begun to learn three startling things. First, I knew it was Jayton's first football team, but it wasn't. Second, I knew my brother was on the first string from the start, but he wasn't. Third, I knew I had it all remembered well, but I didn't. I thought I would have remembered all of the games, but I didn't (I never heard of Fluvanna, I think, until I read the account in the *Chronicle*, though I know now that it's down in Scurry County, not too far from Snyder).

No, *four* startling things. I learned to wonder why I had stored them all so in my mind and lingered over them all these years. They weren't heroes. They were boys, and they are gone, and that's all right, and I'm alone, and that's all right.

But there's more Jayton Jaybird football. The *Chronicle* for September 17, 1942, tells me that "the Jayton Jay Birds have begun their football work outs with some eighteen boys reporting." I don't recognize any of the names: my brother's contemporaries are all gone, and those who would have been my classmates are still too young. The paper for September 24, 1942, notifies me that the first game of the season is scheduled for two P.M., Friday, September 25. "The Jayton Jay Birds will open their football season Friday afternoon on the local field. They face a swarm of Hornets from Aspermont." The next week's paper (October 1, 1942) reports on the game:

> Jaybirds Trampled by Aspermont Hornets
> The Jayton Jaybirds lost their opening football game to a fast light team of "Hornets" from Aspermont. The Jaybirds allowed two touchdowns in the first half to go down fighting to the tune of 13 to 0.
> A return match is scheduled for the near future and with the addition of another coach the local boys will be out for revenge fully prepared.

By now, I am uncertain how to spell the team's name. Sometimes it's Jay Birds. Sometimes it's Jaybirds. At any rate, I have no more news of the 1942 season: issues of the *Chronicle* that might have told of the other games are missing from my file.

And I can't report on the 1943 season. Only one issue of the *Chronicle* survived as far as where I am, that for April 9.

I have no issues at all for 1944. So goes the Jaybirds' 1944 football season.

But I learn that "The Jaybirds Are At It Again Full Speed" in September, 1945. "The Jayton Jaybirds opened their football practice September 4 with 26 men reporting for workout," says the September 13 paper. A list of nineteen names, not twenty-six, follows. These are my contemporaries now, and perhaps I should remember all or most, but I recognize only two: one is Bobby Ray Stanley; the other is Jimmy Matthews, my best friend of former times. Another item in the same issue of the *Chronicle* announces that the Jaybirds will play their first game of the season in September against the Dickens Owls.

Dickens won, 19-6, the September 20 paper says, but that's not the most notable news of the game. First, I learned finally that Jimmy played center. Second, and more: "At the end of the third quarter, Hamilton of Jayton slapped down a punt which was recovered by Matthews of Jayton who made a run of 70 yards for a touchdown." I also learn that he played the whole game.

The next notice comes on September 27, 1945. I learn that the Jaybirds will play the McAdoo Hornets on Friday.

But the McAdoo game didn't come off—bad weather caused cancellation, so the October 4 paper says. Now the Jaybirds will play Dickens again on Friday, October 5. The same story reveals something else: Jayton has no coach. The team has, nevertheless, "been working very hard this week."

The October 11 issue reports that Jayton will play Patton Springs on Friday.

The October 25 issue announces a game against McAdoo for Friday.

The missing *Chronicles* won't tell me the scores or the circumstances or what Jimmy did.

After the October 25, 1945, notice, there is silence until September 5, 1946. In the meantime, I am far from Jayton, have not thought much about Jayton, would not go back to Jayton again for years. I wish it were not so, Jimmy, for I should have been there to help. In the meantime, after October 25, 1945, and before September 5, 1946, something momentous has happened. I don't know exactly why, and the missing *Chronicles* won't share the discussion and debate with me.

When word comes again about football, in the September 5, 1946 issue, the Jaybirds have already converted to six-man football. They are to play Dickens, Patton Springs, Peacock, McAdoo, Dickens again, Patton Springs again, Peacock again, and McAdoo again.

The September 19 issue tells me more about what Jimmy is doing, and teaches me a little about six-man football:

> JAYTON TEAM TUNING UP FOR FIRST GAME 20TH
> There ae 15 candidates for the 1946 Jayton High School 6-man football team [probably reason enough to convert to six-man style]. The team climaxed the first week of training Monday, September 16, by going through a long scrimmage session. First game is with the Patton sextet on the Jayton field, Friday, September 20, at 2 p.m. The team also took part in a skull practice, learning plays, and elected Jimmy Matthews Captain and Bert Sartain Co-Captain.
>
> Out of the total of 15 candidates, eight can do a fairly good job carrying the ball, and a few others have been in the backfield during practice. Hanford (Shorty) Long is the most versatile member of the team. This mile runner can play all backfield positions, end, or center, as he is needed. He has some speed and is a good broken-field runner. The team is also fortunate in that six ranking backs can also make up the team at a given time. By shifting Hugh Kissick and Shorty Long to the end positions, and Bert Sartain to the center, room is made for Frank Sandell at quarter or half and Melvin Florence and Jimmy Matthews can take the other two positions. Bill Sartain makes an acceptable back, tho he is light, and Johnny Davis can be shifted from end to half. Glendell Underwood and R. A. Moreland get the call for the regular center position, in that order, provided the team does not need a crusher like Bert or Shorty. . . .
>
> When it comes to head-on power, Bert Sartain and Frank Sandell rate highest. Hugh Kissick did very well for a new position at end Monday, and the stocky redhead should go places in interference and tackling. He will be used as end and halfback. Jimmy Matthews and Melvin Florence will be used mostly in the secondary, Melvin at quarter and "Matt" at full. "Matt" and Frank should do a good job on fullback. . . .
>
> Probable starting line-up for Friday: Backfield: Matthews, full, Florence, quarter, Bert Sartain or Sandell, half. Line: Kissick and Long, ends, Bert Sartain or Underwood, center.

I note, incidentally, that there is still no mention of a coach.

Their preparations didn't suffice. The next issue of the *Chronicle,* for September 26, 1945, says that Patton Springs beat them on Friday, 34–0, that Peacock beat them on Wednesday, 44–0.

I should have been there to help you, Jimmy. We'd have done all right. We'd have made it.

My file on Jaybird football ends there.

I began by promising a story of Jaybird football from 1938 to 1946. Those are *my* dates, not any other's—1938 is not *the* beginning, and 1946 is not *the* end. Nineteen thirty-eight is the beginning, 1946 the ending for a narrative in *my* mind of Jaybird football. The narrative I made in my mind is not the narrative the players made over the years, not the narrative the citizens of the town made. Turns out I learned a fifth startling lesson, that I got my narrative wrong, too.

Still: I should have been there to help you, Jimmy. We'd have done all right. We'd have made it.

34

Remember the Names

Once upon a time, long after we moved to the big city, and I don't know when it was, maybe sometime in 1942, maybe early in 1943—the truth is, I don't know—I heard something uncanny on the radio, altogether by chance. I was listening otherwise, maybe to music, maybe to the news, maybe to who knows what, and all of a sudden realized that I was hearing the announcer say that he was going to read something that Mr. L. F. Wade had written for the *Jayton Chronicle*. Maybe it was earlier than I remember, maybe still early 1942, not long after the war started.

What the announcer read, what Mr. Wade wrote, was an incantation, a liturgy in praise of the names that we must not forget. What I remember that time from the radio is an incantation of names—remember the names, remember the names, Mr. Wade seemed to be saying, as I recall the moment—the names of boys, of young men, who'd already been in the Pacific when the war started and were now maybe lost, maybe forever; the names of boys, of young men, who'd soon after gone to war, who were scattered everywhere, who might not return to Jayton. It was an uncanny moment, Jayton made real, boys made real, young men made real, Mr. Wade made real there somehow in the air on the other side of the radio from me.

I have tried, Mr. Wade, tried, tried to remember the names, and I cannot get them right.

Sometimes, when I hear a child's call, say far down the block past the arching green trees, or maybe way over on the next street and down, or maybe just at twilight, I want to go and say his name, or hers, want to go and be her guard, or his, and teach the child safely home. Some-times a child calls, far off, maybe just at twilight. Sometimes I think I know who the child is and maybe where home is, and want to hold her safe, or him, say his name, or hers. Mostly, though, I doubt I can reach that far geography.

35

Nineteen Forty-three

I have only one paper for this year, the *Chronicle* for April 9, 1943, and news is sparse.

I see on the front page that "five more Kent County Boys left this week to take up their duties with Uncle Sam's fighting forces." Frank Hale, Jr., has gone, and so has Billie Hamilton and Jesse Merle Taylor and Arthur Martin and John Martin Johnson. "Each boy was given a testament, a gift from the Jayton Baptist Church." Still on the front page: the Navy Department is urging folks to use V-Mail for Navy personnel. And also on the front page: "FLASH—9:30 a.m. Thursday [the day the *Chronicle* was printed]—A million dollar rain, .65 of an inch and it's still raining. This is the latest on the weather from Jayton."

Inside, I notice that Corporal Forest (Tot) Holley of South Carolina is visiting his folks, Mr. and Mrs. Tom Holley, and Pvt. Billie Suggs spent the weekend with home folks. Kent County is being called on to buy $30,000 in Victory War Bonds. The Texan Theater is showing "Forbidden Trails" on Friday and Saturday, with Buck Jones and Tim McCoy; "Tales of Manhattan" on the Saturday night preview, Sunday, and Monday, with Charles Boyer, Rita Hayworth, Ginger Rogers, Henry Fonda, Charles Laughton, Edward G. Robinson, and George Sanders; and "Call Out the Marines" on Tuesday, Wednesday, and Thursday, with Victor McLaglen and Edmund Lowe.

Over at Gardner Brothers Grocery, flour is up, forty-eight pounds for $2.35, but other prices are holding fairly well—a big can of baking powder for a quarter, with a small can free, good brooms for 39 cents, a gallon of syrup for 75 cents, and two pounds of crackers for 19 cents. B. Schwarz and Son, the dry goods store up in Spur, has an advertisement in the paper, and prices seem to be up a little—ladies' hats run from $2.98 all the way to $7.95. Robinson's grocery doesn't list separate items, just says, "Don't Have Worries," then, "Come to us for your food needs, bring your ration stamps and we will do the rest. By trading here you can be well fed at a minimum cost for quality groceries go farther and thereby cost less in the long run. Bring us your EGGS and buy your poultry feed here and we will show our appreciation in the service given you." Jones Drug and Huls Drug have a joint advertisement: "NOTICE! Due to the shortage of help and other conditions over which we have no control, we are forced to discontinue Curb Service after Sunday, April 11. We take pleasure in serving our customers, but this is one service we are obliged to discontinue."

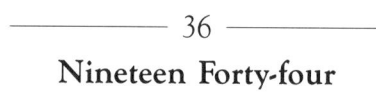

36

Nineteen Forty-four

I have no copies of the *Chronicle* for 1944. I wonder how things were, and what the news was, and what I might have learned from the missing issues.

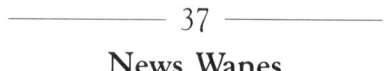

37

News Wanes

My *Chronicle* file runs low in 1945 and 1946, and I am far away, farther, it often seems, than forty-three years would account for. Some things are explained in these last issues; some are not.

WAR NEWS

I learn from the February 15, 1945, paper that C. A. Cheyne has been wounded. He joined the navy in May, 1944, the story says, took boot training at Camp Wallace, Texas, then went to San Diego, then to Hawaii, finally to the Philippines, where he was wounded. The paper says he is doing all right.

In the 1942 *Chronicles* I had learned that Sergeant Q. T. Wade of the marines had been taken prisoner on Wake Island. Now word about him comes again, indirectly, in the February 15 issue. T. Sgt. Charles Holmes of Spur, also a prisoner, has written to his mother in Spur, and the *Chronicle* reproduces the long-delayed letter:

Dearest Mother:

Through the kind permission of the Japanese authorities, I am able to write you again. I am in good health. Tell Mrs. Wade that Q. T. is fine also. He and I are the best of pals. Was glad to get your letters of September 1943 and January and February 1944 and learn that you had heard from me. I have received several letters from my friends. I can't write them now, but they will never be forgotten by me as letters are as welcome almost as freedom. Here in two and one-half years I have learned to live a very simple life and manage to stay in good health. We received four Red Cross parcels, food, clothing and toilet articles. Also these are greatly appreciated. I have nothing but praise for the Red Cross. Hope it won't be too much longer until I'll be sitting in the living room enjoying a good pipe full of tobacco, a good cup of coffee and talking to the family.

Your loving son,
Charles Ardon Holmes

The May 10 *Chronicle* reports that Germany has surrendered, but on the same front page reminds everyone, "This is No Time to Relax," with further information about the seventh war loan drive. On the same page, notice comes that Technician Franklin Jones, whose parents live in Jayton, has been awarded the Bronze Star for meritorious service in military operations in Germany on November 22, 1944: "Technician Fifth Class Jones, while serving as an aid man, entered an area that was under concentrated enemy fire and applied first aid to the wounded men. His exceptional devotion to duty with complete disregard for his own safety, serves as an inspiration to men of his organization."

I learn from the May 24 *Chronicle* that seven more young men have left for service—the war really isn't over—and that Wayne Rose, formerly of Jayton, has been killed in a plane crash while serving in the air corps.

Brief word first appears in the May 31 *Chronicle* that Rex Cox, grandson of Mrs. J. H. Donoho of Jayton, died of wounds received in action in the Philippines. I knew his name from the roster of the 1939 Jaybirds.

The June 7 paper says that Kent County has done its duty in the war loan bond drive: "Good old Kent County has subscribed both her E Bond quota and her overall quota and is now working hard to pull poor old Dickens County out of the hole. As you know because Kent County has no bank, we are tied on to Dickens County and the two are given a quota together. But this grand total is divided, each county given a certain amount of the grand total, and the *Chronicle* just wants the world to know that Kent County has made good with the boys over there. . . ." The same issue reports that Private Clifford Dyer of Camp Hood spent last weekend at home in Jayton with his wife and daughter. The June 14 *Chronicle* says that Ensign Jackie Patton of Pensacola, Florida, has spent a few days with his folks in Jayton. He was the quarterback on the 1938–39 Jaybirds.

Under the headline "Sad News," I begin to learn more from the June 21, 1945, *Chronicle*. H. J. Whatley, Jr., of the "lost battalion," didn't get away into the mountains as that Dutch officer had hoped:

> Sunday, June 17. Sheriff H. J. Whatley was notified by wire that his only son, H. J. Whatley, Jr., had died in a Jap prison of war camp, and every heart in Jayton was saddened by the tragic news.
>
> If our information is correct, H. J., Jr. was captured on the island of Java just after the war started. For months everyone hoped he and his company had escaped to the mountains on the island and would be able to hold out until rescued, but eventually it was learned through the Red Cross that he had been captured. Since that time, he has only been heard from once, until the death message was received Sunday.
>
> Mr. Whatley has the sincere sympathy of all in his bereavement but nothing that any one can do or say, can take the place in his life filled by his son.
>
> H. J. was a fine, upstanding young man. He liked everyone and everyone liked him. He had a big smile and a happy greeting for his friends, young or old, every time he met them. And we will never forget how many the times he barged into the *Chronicle* office and sang out, "Hello Editor! Need another printer today?"
>
> We hate to think how much he suffered while a Jap prisoner for those many months before he died, which is just one more reason we believe that Japan as a nation should be utterly destroyed.

How is it, I have sometimes wondered and still do, to pray for the well-being of a child who is already dead? How is it to learn that you have done so? Harder, I expect, to be the child.

But the others begin to come home. The June 28 paper says that Tommie Simmons is home after serving twenty-one months with the medical corps in the Forty-fifth Division. He had been reported missing briefly, and then it was learned that he had been captured with others by the Germans.

The issue for July 5 says that Lt. Newton Lewis of Jayton has been awarded the Bronze Star and Oak Leaf Cluster for meritorious service against the enemy on September 20, 1944, but the place is not given.

The same paper reprints a letter to Mr. Whatley from the adjutant general, confirming the wire notice of the young man's death.

Pfc. Barney Cumbie has come home to Aspermont, the July 12, 1945, paper reports. He trained at Camp Roberts, California, then went to New Caledonia, then to Australia, then to Burma, where he was in active combat, then came home by way of India, the Red Sea, the Suez Canal, the Mediterranean, Gibraltar, and the Atlantic. Now, "I want to go on to Jayton," he told his father. "That's all I lack going around the world."

The *Chronicle* reports on July 19, 1945, that Jesse Ward Holley is home after three years of service overseas.

The August 2 issue, in commentary on the front page, reckons that "Japan is Licked. That's a settled fact and the mop-up is getting under way. The cut throat bunch of heathen gangsters, who declare they prefer death to surrender, are now in the same position as Germany was when our force swept across the Rhine." The August 9 paper has another front-page commentary, this on the destructive power of the atomic bomb. The same issue reports that Pfc. Tom Bill Fowler, United States Marine Corps, is on furlough, visiting home.

On August 16, 1945, the *Chronicle* carries this headline:

THE WAR IS OVER THANK GOD
JAPAN SURRENDERS—UNCONDITIONALLY

It isn't altogether over, not for some who are still scattered around the world, and it never was over for others. The September 13 *Chronicle* says Robert Wade, now in the field artillery in Manila, has just been promoted to captain. The same paper carries more word about Rex Cox:

STAFF SERGEANT REX R. COX
The following letter received by Mrs. Betty Marie Cox, wife of Staff Sergeant Rex R. Cox, who died of wounds received in action at Balete Pass, Luzon.

My Dear Mrs. Cox:
I am writing to express my sincere sympathies on the death of your husband, Staff Sergeant Rex R. Cox, who died of wounds received in action at Balete Pass, Luzon, Philippine Islands on 1 May 1945. There is little I can say to assuage your sorrow, but you would undoubtedly like to know some of the circumstances surrounding his death.
Our Company had the mission of seizing a piece of commanding ground that was strongly defended by the enemy. Your hus-

band's squad had the mission of flanking a machine-gun position. He was leading his squad along a densely vegetated trail when hidden snipers opened fire on him and his squad. Rex was working his way toward where he could best lead his squad. As he was moving forward, he was wounded by one of the snipers. We rushed him to the battalion aid station, where despite the attention of the battalion surgeon, he died of his wounds.

You can well be proud of your husband and his courage in fighting the enemy. His comrades still remember him and speak highly of him and his soldierly ability.

It is indeed regretful that it has been necessary for our fine young men to sacrifice their lives for our country, but we are proud of these men and are very grateful for what they have given, resolving that they shall not have died in vain.

Rex was buried with full military honors in the United States Armed Forces Cemetery at Sant Barbara, Pangassinan Province, Luzon, Philippine Islands. The cemetery has been landscaped and rows of palm trees enhance its solemn beauty. It is well cared for by the daily attention of several caretakers and shall be so long as an American soldier is buried there.

Your husband will be well remembered by all the men and officers of the company. We all miss the fine friend we had and all wish to express their deepest regret at the passing of one of our comrades and join in expressing to you our sincerest sentiments.

> Respectfully yours,
> George R. Bitterly
> 1st Lt., 35th Infantry
> Commanding

The September 27, 1945, *Chronicle* says that Halley Wade has returned to duty in San Diego after spending leave with his folks. The October 4 paper reports that Sergeant Don Cox, grandson of Mrs. J. H. Donoho of Jayton, has been liberated. He had been a prisoner of the Japanese since the fall of the Philippines. The paper also reports that Sergeant Q. T. Wade has been liberated.

Then on October 4 the *Chronicle* carries the announcement of a big homecoming celebration in Wichita Falls on October 28–29 for members of the "lost battalion," their families and friends, and everyone who wants to come. The survivors had been in a Japanese stockade in the Philippines, but now they have come home. Further notice appears on October 25:

OFFICIAL HOMECOMING OF "THE LOST BATTALION"
Wichita Falls, Oct. 13 – To apply the familiar words of their service branch's universally known marching song, members of the

131st Field Artillery Lost Battalion of Java will "over hill, over dale, hit the dusty trail" for Wichita Falls next Sunday and Monday, October 28 and 29.

For the survivors of this Texas born and trained unit, all roads will lead on those two days to Wichita Falls, where an official homecoming proclaimed by Gov. Coke Stevenson awaits them.

Coming back from the oblivion of more than 1200 days in Jap hands these hardy veterans of the luckless Java campaign will receive heartfelt tribute from a large delegation of national, state, and local public figures led by Maj. Gen. Fred L. Walker and Gov. Stevenson.

The November 29 paper carries two stories as "Local Servicemen Relate Stories of Jap Prison Life." Private Chester Burks of Girard was wounded and taken prisoner on Corregidor and held for the duration of the war. Sgt. Don Cox was captured at Bataan, went on the "Death March," and was also held for the duration. On the same front page a story appears with this headline, "Air Armada Is Useless, Now Being Chopped Up":

> Washington—The bulk of the government's investment in wartime airplanes, amounting to many billions of dollars, became worthless with the end of the war. As a result, thousands of airplanes are being chopped up and heaved into smelters for the scrap metal that can be salvaged.

The *Chronicle* for February 21, 1946, carries this story:

> WHATLEY-HANCOCK, NAME SELECTED FOR LEGION POST
> Last Thursday night veterans of World War I and II from Kent County met in called session and by unanimous vote selected the name Whatley-Hancock for their post.
> H. J. Whatley, son of Sheriff Whatley, according to word from the War Department, died in a Japanese prison camp.
> Curtis Hancock, grandson of Mrs. W. S. Hancock, was reported killed in action when the plane he was piloting was lost on a mission in the Southwest Pacific Campaign. . . .

LOCAL NEWS

Maude Brown of Gilpin was shopping in Jayton on Tuesday, May 8, according to the May 10 paper. Is that Maude Adele Brown, I wonder, who was in my room at school?

I learn from the May 24 paper that Uncle Martin and Aunt Mary and Uncle Bill and my Grandma Corder visited in Jayton over the weekend. The June 7 paper says the Sproules family has moved back to Jay-ton from Lubbock. The last house we lived in back in 1939 was next door to theirs; I learned to play Monopoly with Bobby.

On July 5, John J. Van Pell of Lubbock, districk manager of the Office of Defense Transportation, is urging folks to conserve their cars because "it will be at least three years before many millions of private car owners and prospective car owners who want new automobiles, will be able to get them."

I guess Jimmy Cox's family moved away, too. I notice in the July 5 paper that Billy Glenn Vencil has been to visit him in Stamford.

The *Chronicle* for July 19, 1945, carries this story:

> SHERIFF WHATLEY CAPTURES TRAVELING BOOZE PEDDLER
> Late last Friday evening a certain party, whom Sheriff Whatley had been keeping an eye on for some time, drove his jalopy into Jayton and carelessly parked it in the center of the business dis-trict of the town. After parking his car, the party driving it got out and entered the nearest grocery store and while he was inside the sheriff drove up in his car and parked it beside the booze wagon. Getting out the sheriff calmly awaited the return of the suspect. When he came out of the grocery store, the sheriff engaged him in casual talk and while the conversation was going on the sheriff reached through the window of the car which was down, and lifted the cover from the load of booze, after which he took charge of the driver, the car and the contents of the car, over the protests of the owner.
> Later the party made bond and went on his way, but the sher-iff kept the booze, quite a liberal amount, and now has it under lock and key.

In the same paper I notice that Nannie Beth Rice (not Maddux now) has been for a visit to Lubbock.

By his own account in the August 2 paper, the editor has made the bust of a lifetime: "After spending a half century in the printing business we made the bust of a lifetime last week when we let a half page of advertisement get by without the store name. We offer our re-grets to our readers and to the advertiser, B. Schwarz and Son, Spur, Texas, and we hope we will not make another such error again for an-other 50 years."

I see by the August 9 paper that Jimmy Cox came up from Stam-ford for a visit with Billy Glenn Vencil, and the August 16 paper—the same issue that says the war is over—tells me that Bobbie Nell Fuller has gotten married, on August 10 at the Baptist parsonage in Jayton.

The *Chronicle* says on September 20 that the Office of Labor has approved a wage ceiling of $1.35 a hundred for snapping or pulling cotton and $2.25 for well-picked clean cotton. The next week's paper reports that President Truman has signed a bill turning the clocks back to standard time from daylight saving or war time. The November 1 paper says that the first new post-war car, a Ford, is available at Black Motor Company, and WTU has just received the first post-war model Frigidaire. However, according to the November 22 paper, bacon is still scarce and will be until spring, and the prospect for men's clothes is poor: "With shelf stocks at the lowest point since the war began, clothing manufacturers held out a little hope for improved supplies of suits and coats for men but cautioned that production hinges on getting more rayon for linings."

I learn from an account in the September 5, 1946, issue of the *Chronicle* that Mr. and Mrs. John Jones of Brandon, Mississippi, have been back for a Jones family reunion. I guess that's Don's family.

From the September 26, 1946, paper I learn that Kent County has voted to stay dry.

Crops and Weather

My news is pretty sparse. The paper reports on Thursday, June 7, 1945, that "Monday evening between 6 and 7 o'clock practically all of Jayton kept a close eye on the cyclone which struck the north western part of the county. . . ." Several houses were destroyed. The August 30 paper carries a nice report on the work of the Duck Creek Soil Conservation District. The first bale of cotton came in on August 28, so the September 13 paper says. The October 4 issue reports a good rain.

Later, we're talking drought again. By August 15, 1946, the *Chronicle* reports that Texas is sweltering in the worst drought of the past ten years. Somehow, that seems unlikely, considering what they said in 1937 and 1938. The last issue of the *Chronicle* that I have, the paper for December 12, 1946, reports a good rain.

Sports and Entertainment

The news here is skimpy, too.

I see by the October 4, 1945, paper that Floyd Blair has bought the Texan Theater, and that he and his family will live in the "apartment connected with the theater." I wonder where it was—maybe behind the screen area, or upstairs near the projection booth?

On February 21, 1946, I learn that the Jayton boys have won the district basketball championship. Jimmy Matthews is on the team. I also learn that the theater is now under new management. I don't believe the theater business was too steady in Jayton some years. In the next week's paper, I see that the boys' basketball team has gone on to defeat Aspermont, which was champion in its district: "Patton, Pearson, and Long from Jayton, working with patience and skill, feeding, faking and firing the ball to Stanley and Matthews, demonstrated basketball that few high school teams can boast." Matthews was high-point man. In the April 4, 1946, issue I learn that Jimmy was third in the 440-yard dash in the district track meet and tied for first in the high jump.

SCHOOL NEWS

On August 30, 1945, the *Chronicle* announces that school will open on September 3. Among the faculty listed, I find Mrs. Fowler and Mrs. Jay. The September 6 paper says that the junior class has elected officers. Lucille Robinson is president. Olive Engledow is secretary-treasurer.

News falls off now, and I don't hear anything more until the fall of 1946, when the ones I knew are seniors. When the *Chronicle* announces on September 5, 1946, that school will open on September 9 and lists the faculty, Mrs. Fowler and Mrs. Jay are still there, but I don't recognize any other names. On September 19, 1946, I get word that the seniors have elected Billy Glenn Vencil president, Olive Engledow secretary. That's all I know about school.

THE MARKET REPORT

On February 15, 1945, Gardner Brothers Grocery has a gallon of ribbon cane syrup for $1.25, a one-pound jar of pork and beans for 15 cents, coffee for 16 cents a pound, and will give 32 cents in trade for a dozen eggs. Flour is up a little everywhere—a fifty-pound bag costs $2.38 or thereabouts.

On September 20, 1945, flour is still about the same, $2.35 for fifty pounds at Gardners, but coffee is up, a three-pound jar for $1.09. A pound of grapes is 15 cents. At the dry goods store, men's leather coats and jackets range from $12.50 to $19.75, plaid shirts are $1.90, blankets are $1.35, dresses run from $7.95 to $22.50, and a chenille bath set costs $3.95.

In the November 29, 1945, paper, I notice that Mr. Bradley of WTU is now in Matador.

JAYTON

In the last issue of the *Chronicle* that I have, for December 12, 1946, this item appears on the front page:

> TOWN NAMED FOR HIS FATHER
> *Abilene There When Jayton Got Its Start*
> Cowboy, banker, town-founder, ranchman, realtor, epitomize the colorful career of Joe Jay, real estate, rental, and fire insurance dealer of 1150 Vine.
> Born in Brownwood April 10, 1878, son of Mr. and Mrs. D. N. Jay, frontier folk, Jay indistinctly remembers passing through the swaddling-cloth tent city of Abilene, as he moved on with his parents to Kent County in 1884 to establish a stock farm. The elder Jay came from Ohio, stopped for a while in Kansas before lighting in Texas. He died November 11, 1919, at the age of 88, after the thriving town of Jayton, Kent County, was named for him.
> "In those days," Mr. Jay observed, "only a few trappers and buffalo hunters were in Kent County." . . .

38

Blinders

I have wondered time and again about the missing issues of the *Chronicle*, about the missing days, weeks, years, about what I would have found that I remembered, what I would have found that I saw or knew and forgot, what I would have found that I never saw or knew.

About some things, I could have learned more if I had looked beyond the *Chronicle*. I have been, for example, curious to learn more about Jeff Brown. He's buried in the Jayton cemetery, and I cited earlier the inscription on his tombstone. I had the story of his death from my father, and I don't know where he learned it, for we had long since left Jayton before Jeff Brown died. He died, as I recall the story, on a bombing raid over Europe. An older sergeant, he had promised the young man in the ball turret that he would not abandon him if they got into trouble. Sure enough, as the story goes, their plane was hit, and they couldn't get the ball turret open. Other members of the crew apparently bailed out, and as the story ended, Jeff Brown had kept his promise and was stomping on the ball turret, trying to the end to get the young man out.

I became especially curious about the story when, some months ago, President Reagan told a visiting group an almost identical story. Apparently no one present thought until later to inquire how it was known, if no one else who survived was present, what the sergeant was doing when the plane went down. I never thought to inquire, either. I wrote to Headquarters, United States Air Force Historical Research Center, at Maxwell Air Force Base in Alabama. The reply follows:

> In reference to your 27 October 1987 letter, we regret that we cannot assist you with information about a T. Sgt. Jeff Brown. We do not maintain service records on individuals and therefore, have no way of identifying T. Sgt. Brown. We, however, maintain unit records and could possibly assist you with information on his missions and death if you could provide the number and name of the unit to which he was assigned and the exact date on which he was killed.
>
> We have contacted the Memorial Affairs Division of the Casualty and Memorial Affairs Directorate, in Alexandria, Virginia and have learned that the first name was probably a nickname since the only Jeff Brown listed in its files was buried in Iowa.
>
> We have enclosed a "Steps to Follow . . ." worksheet to assist you in securing further information.

But I haven't done so. I did call Cornelia Cheyne at Kent County courthouse in Jayton, and she remembered that Sergeant Brown's sister still lived in Jayton. I called her and learned that his name was Andrew Jefferson Brown.

I haven't inquired further. That's another story, and I will look later. For now, I chose not to look beyond the *Chronicle*, which means that I keep on wondering about the missing issues, missing days, weeks, years, about what I would have found that I remembered, what I would have found that I saw or knew and forgot, what I would have found that I never saw or knew.

But I have looked in the *Chronicles* that I have, hoping maybe to find myself or others, failing, have looked here, there, yonder, but not everywhere. When you look everywhere, look back or out or sideways or in or down or up, wherever that is, you come at last, in any

direction, to the place of which there is no knowledge, of which there can be no knowledge, come to that place but not into it, come only to abut it. But I don't know how to look everywhere and can't see everywhere, were I to come close. I have looked, hoping maybe to find myself or others, failing.

And I'm not there, nor are others, and the places where we were aren't there, not there in the issues I have, not there in the issues that are missing. It's at any rate a search for what is not, for the thing that never happened, for the place that never was. That doesn't mean there is no reason to look. I'm also there, and the others are, and the places are, and there are always reasons to look, to get into as many situations for seeing as possible. We ache for home even if it never was; we always know better and don't, and love a place—or don't love it—even if it never was.

Does nostalgia, I wonder, seize us all the more sadly and immediately in times of rapid change, when the new rushes at us far sooner than we can comprehend? In the wilderness, manna for a moment was not enough, and the people for a moment fondly remembered Egypt, fondly remembered the fish and the cucumbers and the melons and the leeks and the onions and the garlic. We convert other times and places into sites of significance even when we did not see them well, and then misremembered.

And we mostly don't see that well, for the place where we are at any moment puts blinders on us, and what we don't see well, we then go out and misremember.

My own memory fails, God knows, often enough, and I have demonstrated that it fails, God knows, often enough; have demonstrated, too, that before memory failed, perception went awry. What I think I see now, Nicholas Christopher writes in "Quatrains for Sunlight,"

> . . . already may have disappeared,
> transposed—like Rome's power—to Byzantium,
> and the light on this summer morning no more
> than a filter for my misperceptions, a screen.

I come, too, to distrust the record. If I wasn't there when and where by *any* kind of reckoning I should have been—at Trades Day, later First Saturday, at barrel races and rodeos right there in Jayton, at county meets, at football games, at softball games, especially softball games, then how in hell can I be sure I was there when they say I was or when I might have been? How am I to explore, if I can't find the site, the digs? I haven't located myself, or others, or the sites where I might dig to find some telling shard.

Others seem sure. I come upon autobiographers and chroniclers of their time who seem blessed with total recall, who are praised for total recall (among recent practitioners, Arthur Miller and Annie Dillard come to mind). I don't doubt that their recall, or ours, is total—we all have total recall. We are always writing the novel that is our life, the narrative that gives us shape, or misshapes us. Psychoanalysts are editors first, if need be, then novelists; they wait upon us, assisting as editors, to make a coherent narrative, or if not a coherent narrative, then a narrative we can live in. If we cannot, they write it for us. We all have total recall. We live upon and through memory.

Whether our memory is accurate by any measure other than our own—say, by the *Jayton Chronicle*—is quite another matter. Mostly it's not. Mine isn't.

The culture's memory fails, too, or we don't pay enough attention to notice and then to remember. Lionel Tiger, in *The Manufacture of Evil*, subtitled *Ethics, Evolution, and the Industrial Revolution*, suggests that mankind leapt into modernity some three centuries ago. He does not seem to notice that we are *always jumping into modernity*, every soul, every generation, always shifting from the pastoral (even if it lasts only a moment) to the urban, always having an Industrial Revolution in every life, in every generation.

That is not to say that we always repeat history. But wo do make our small versions of acts we have all always undertaken. To the great archetypal *character models* and their sometime reenactment in us, we are always adding the small reenactment of great archetypal *actions, movements.* We are always, if we notice, in exodus, *volkswanderung,* always, if we notice, in an age of discovery, or upon the rim of discovery, always making, or trying to make that leap into modernity, always feeling the loss that the leap into modernity brings, always recovering, or trying to recover, always on the edge of Holocaust, or there, soul by soul, generation by generation.

I will not presume to equate private sadness, even private desolation and destruction, with events that are beyond being great public tragedies. Even as we privately enter our own trials, we use failed memory to revise such experiences as the Holocaust into simpler forms so that what we might have learned is lost as it is routinized. Still, we make our minor exodus, our own leap into modernity, and, sometimes, our own Holocaust.

I have sometimes joked, sometimes rationalized, that I could never write the Great American Novel (and I can't) because I was never seduced by my black nanny or my blond aunt, never lived in New York, never hit anyone in anger, never went to war, wasn't part of the proletariat in the thirties or of the peace movement of the sixties and seventies —never, in other words, participated in any great *moment* or *movement.* But of course I did (though I wtill can't write that novel): I was in a great exodus, knew somehow a vague hope accompanied by vague regret, knew a loss—of exactly what I cannot say—and still find myself trying to remember the leeks and the onions and the garlic.

But perception fails and memory misspeaks. We have to get into many places to be able to see and to remember, and we'll still not be able to see and to remember. When we stop, when we stop looking, when we settle into one place for looking, we put on blinders. They focus our vision wonderfully in one direction, but turn us blind otherwise.

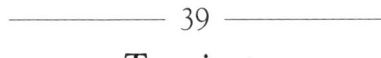

39

Transients

Once in the spring of 1937, I stayed home from school sick, and a hard, dark sandstorm blew in, though the sun was still there above it. That afternoon, when my brother got off the bus and started home, the sand was blowing so hard that he lost his way and had to backtrack to find home. Later, he swore to me that the sun was shining above the dust and the dust was thick, and he saw his shadow in the air beside him, and I believed him, and I still do. But even if I have it all wrong, brother, we were not just shadows in the air, not shadows, brother, not shadows, not transients passing while no one noticed.

And yet we are transients, brother, ghosts, most of the time invisible.

I have often felt invisible, even if it's odd to be invisible and still imagine that you *feel* it, have often felt unworthy of notice even while I wanted more notice than the world could ever give even while I didn't want notice. I have often felt that I might grow fuzzy around the edges and disappear while others were watching, but not paying much attention, have sometimes gone, I want to imagine, in search of evidence for myself and found none. I have often, at the same time, been arrogant, I hope unaware.

Arrogant, I have turned others into transients, declared them ghosts, therefore invisible. I have valorized myself, wanting, claiming identity for myself among them, against them, with, through, and in them, those others who wanted to be identities. I have made them into my thoughts, my stories. Even while I wanted to celebrate them, to know them — Mr. Wade and Peggy Sue Robinson and Jeff Brown and Curtis Hancock and H. J. Whatley and Jimmy Matthews and Don Jones and Mr. Parker and Cornelia Cheyne and Bobbie Nell Fuller and Maude Adele Brown and Billy Glenn Vencil and Grandpa Corder and Jimmy Cox and Grandma Corder and Grandpa Durham and Mr. Coons and the man who went as far as he could and then lay down under a tree and died and all the rest of them — I have instead held them in my head, made them into my thoughts, my stories, have not known them as their thoughts, their stories.

Any small exodus we make is always out from ourselves, and mostly not far, though some of us travel strange, dark distances.

At Abernathy's Restaurant and Bar on Berry Street, I watch a little girl at the table across the way and take her away from herself into my memories of my children. But she is real over there, *and* transient, a ghost already flown into my mind, and perhaps I hear her call, far off in both worlds, or far down the block past the arching green trees, or maybe way over on the next street and down, or maybe just at twilight, or at the table across the way. I want to go and be her guard, or sometimes his, and teach the child safely home. Sometimes a child calls, far off, maybe just at twilight. Sometimes, I know who the child is and know the child is, without me, and where home is without me, and even if I'm a ghost, want still to hold her safe, or him.

But the little girl at the table across the way in Abernathy's Restaurant and Bar is real. She is herself. She's not a mere interpretation, a ghost in my mind, herself already forgotten. And she is a ghost, already captured in my mind.

And I am real, brother, and you are real, and the places are real, though wind and water have worn them beyond what I have known. You are real, and I am real. We remember. We aren't shadows in the air.

And we are. We're transients, ghosts, mere interpretations somewhere else, already forgotten. We're transients, brother, and that's all right.

—— 40 ——

Color and Distance in Kent County, Texas

The tumbleweeds were loose in Kent County on Saturday, January 31, 1987. I had gone back to look, or to see what was already in my mind. I saw them careening across tilled fields, across wide uncultivated stretches, deep with distance. I saw a tumbleweed bouncing mostly toward the north along the street where the theater—called the PALACE or the KENT or the TEXAN, but never the TEXAS—once stood, just up from Gardner's Grocery, just down from Huls Drug, though all are gone now. Caught, the tumbleweeds defined the fence rows down the distance where I couldn't see the wires. They played along the yards and piled against the houses on Cemetery Road. One tumbleweed caught under the table at the picnic area where I took my lunch, some three miles north from Jayton along the road to Spur, where Putoff Canyon goes down from the road into the blue distance. As I drove from Jayton toward Swenson, a tumbleweed rolled and bounced toward me along the highway, jumped lightly against the bumper of the car, scurried along the hood, skittered up my windshield, and scratched its way over my head and down the back of the car. A solitary tumbleweed bounced and rolled and twisted across the cemetery.

The wind was hard and gusting harder. It had blown a film of dust over the top newspaper I took from the rack in front of the grocery store in Aspermont. At Putoff Canyon, it wanted me to hold every-

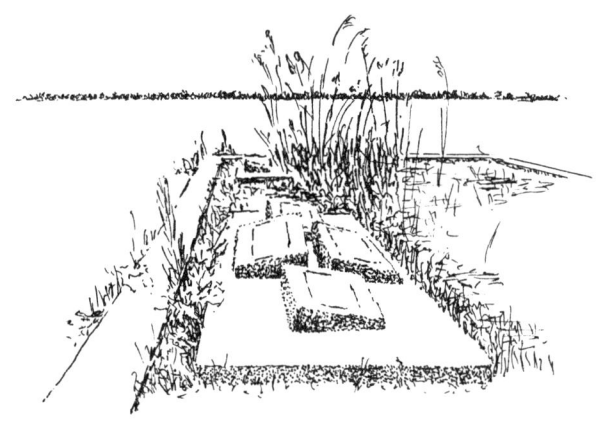

thing down instead of eating my lunch. I weighted my napkin with the can of viennas, held the wrapping from the cheese down with my pocket knife, guarded even the heavier pickle jar against the gusts, wedged my plastic glass of cold cheap white wine inside the cooler so that it wouldn't tilt or blow.

In the cemetery, the wind made the wires sing a lonesome tune.

I know that wires don't sing. I know that tumbleweeds don't feel lonesome. A tumbleweed, the dictionary says, is only a "plant that breaks away from its roots in the autumn and is driven about by the wind as a light rolling mass." But tumbleweeds look lonesome. They make lonesomeness in your mind. If they don't feel lonesome, they are like lonesome, perhaps because so much — so obviously — like ourselves, transients, loosened, whipped about, dodging ahead of the wind, while the wind changes, reshapes, everything behind them, and everything is gone.

Only the thick lower walls of the oil mill remain, and nothing is left of the railroad depot except the concrete foundation and the shell of a cistern. Of seven houses my family lived in during those years, five are gone. The dry goods store on the square is gone, and Jones Drug and Gardner's Grocery and Huls Drug and the theater, by whatever name. A new schoolhouse has replaced the one I knew. Grandpa's farmhouse is gone. The Gilpin post office/service station/grocery is deserted.

The Hagins farm rots. No, it doesn't rot yet. It's only otherwise than I remember, therefore alien to me. But the house is empty, running to ruin.

About ten steps beyond what used to be the Lowrance place on the edge of town, the Croton Breaks begin. The wind and water that made the canyons I remember didn't end their work to keep my memory whole. Erosion goes on being erosion, and nothing looked right, even when I walked deeper into the broken country. Near where the house was, the owner has been busy with a grader, has filled and pushed and shoved and covered, has even made a little dam to hold some water, has changed the shape of the earth I thought I knew.

After I walked in the canyons and through the cemetery and watched the tumbleweeds, I headed back to Aspermont and the Hickman Motel so I could make an early start home in the morning. Out of Jayton, down through the shinnery and on, I drove past Uncle Jack Kidd's old place and the rise where the Center View Church was, and the school below it, gone too, and on, to the bridge over the Salt Fork of the Brazos. I guess that's my favorite place to look at the Double Mountains. You can see them from lots of places—from the cemetery even, from the cow lot on the Lowrance place that used to be the yard of the little house where we lived. And farther, when you leave Putoff Canyon heading south into Jayton, you can see them; the highway is angled so that it seems to aim right for Jayton, with the water tower on the right, and on straight into the middle of the Double Mountains. But looking from the bridge, I think, is best.

I begin at last, though not entirely, to understand why they're blue and why they loom so large from almost anywhere you look in Kent County or Stonewall County. They're always blue, a startling and mysterious blue, until you get within a couple of miles of the lower slopes. I thought blue was a condition of existence, and I guess it is: my friend tells me that what lies between the Double Mountains and me—and oh, so much lies between me and the Double Mountains—refracts light and air and time and turns the mountains blue.

But I hadn't begun until yesterday to understand—and still don't, not entirely—why they seem so high, so big, there on the horizon of my life. On my desk I have a photograph of the Double Mountains and a sketch, both made at the same place, the Brazos bridge. In the sketch, the mountains dominate the scene. In the photograph, they're blue, yes, but low and unprepossessing. The photograph image, another friend tells me, is pretty much like the image on my retina, but then

my retina lies to my brain, or my brain doesn't want to hear the story my retina tells. They look larger in the sketch, apparently, because, looking without the camera, we take distance cues into account and maintain some size constancy inside our heads, and the Double Mountains are always high on the horizon. But the camera will not take notice of distance cues. The photographer who wants to show how we think we perceive a full harvest moon will have to use a telephoto lens, or else the moon will look much smaller than we think we perceive it. I saw the Double Mountains, retina caught an image of them, but I changed their size inside my head. I saw them as they were and as they weren't and as they were and as they will be.

I don't know what looking tells you, but looking from the Brazos bridge is good.

A little way up from the bridge, I turned off Highway 380 south onto Farm Road 2211 for Peacock. On through Peacock—it didn't take long—I followed 2211 south until it turned east toward Aspermont. There, I turned west on the narrow dirt road, drove to Double Mountain Cemetery, then turned south again. After a way the road turned twisty but mostly west, and finally there was a last turn to the south. There, the road peters out, and I was as close as you can get to the Double Mountains unless you walk, and that's still a way. They're not blue when you get close.

I stopped and looked a while and came away, drove back along the dirt road to a rise where I could see the Double Mountains whole and clear. I stopped the car, opened the back and the ice chest there, poured another plastic glass of the cheap cold white wine, and looked again. Already, in this near distance, they'd gone blue again. I drank the wine and poured another glass. Down along the slope before me, I saw a lone tumbleweed bouncing and twisting before the wind. Do we, too, blow before the wind to lodge under some picnic table, to skitter across some cemetery, to catch along a fence line and define it?

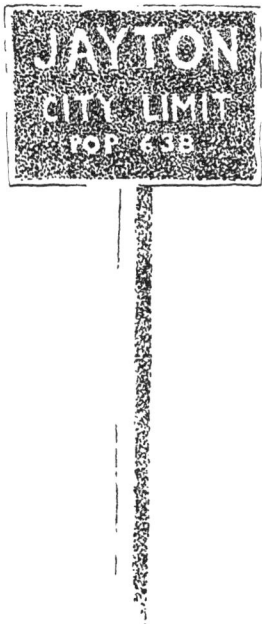

I looked and looked and wondered whether I'd go to Jayton any more, or to what was Grandpa's farm, or to the canyons, or to see the Double Mountains. Then, I didn't much think so. Perhaps some day. I don't know. I probably will.

		DATE DUE		